THE PHYSICAL BODY, THE SPIRITUAL BODY

ainsley chalmers

BALBOA.
PRESS

A DIVISION OF HAY HOUSE

Balboa Press books may be ordered through booksellers or by contacting:

Balboa Press
A Division of Hay House
1663 Liberty Drive
Bloomington, IN 47403
www.balboapress.com.au
1 (877) 407-4847

Because of the dynamic nature of the Internet, any web addresses or
links contained in this book may have changed since publication and
may no longer be valid. The views expressed in this work are solely those
of the author and do not necessarily reflect the views of the publisher,
and the publisher hereby disclaims any responsibility for them.

The author of this book does not dispense medical advice or prescribe the use
of any technique as a form of treatment for physical, emotional, or medical
problems without the advice of a physician, either directly or indirectly. The
intent of the author is only to offer information of a general nature to help you
in your quest for emotional and spiritual well-being. In the event you use any
of the information in this book for yourself, which is your constitutional right,
the author and the publisher assume no responsibility for your actions.

Any people depicted in stock imagery provided by Thinkstock are models,
and such images are being used for illustrative purposes only.
Certain stock imagery © Thinkstock.

Printed in the United States of America.

ISBN: 978-1-4525-2498-6 (sc)
ISBN: 978-1-4525-2499-3 (e)

Balboa Press rev. date: 09/17/2014

This book is dedicated to the memory of my wife Denise who led me to Jesus Christ and went to be with the Lord in December 1991.

It is also dedicated to my children Joanne, Nicole, Jacqueline, John (deceased) and my grandchildren Joshua, Matthew, Isaac, George, Charles and Rubi Rose (great grandchild).

I would also like to acknowledge the many who have helped me in my Christian walk and finally to Creation Ministry International who helped by tying up a lot of theological loose ends in my journey with the Lord thereby helping to increase my faith in him.

To the ideas and inspiration for this book I give God the glory because without his help it would not have been.

CONTENTS

CHAPTER 1

INTRODUCTION

I was asked to speak to a Christian group on Acquired Immune Deficiency Syndrome (AIDS) because of my research activity in this area. The plan was to give a general *address* on the scientific aspects of AIDS such as how HIV virus (Human Immunodeficiency Virus) kills immune cells in the body, the epidemiology and spread of the disease. However whilst writing this talk, it seemed that the scientific /medical aspects of AIDS had a spiritual counterpart (this aspect is explored further in the chapter on "Genes").

The concept that the physical and spiritual may be interrelated was a new concept to me. It probably would be true to say that most people including scientists believe that the disciplines of Science and Theology are two separate, unrelated (sometimes antagonistic) disciplines. Science is centered mainly on the physical or seeable dimension and Theology on the invisible or spiritual. The main area they meet, or rather clash, are in the ethical domain such as in vitro fertilization, stem cell research, cloning, abortion,euthanasia, evolution vs creationism and possibly others. However in scripture we find the apostle Paul had spoken on the physical/spiritual connection in his letter to the Corinthians (1 Cor 15: 44-49) which says in verse 44: "It was sown a natural body; it is raised a spiritual body. There is a natural body and there is a spiritual body". This scripture changed the boundaries of my scientific and theological thinking allowing further scientific/spiritual insights to come and some of these are expressed

1

in this book. In other words, my experiences in the scientific/medical area appeared to have a spiritual counterpart to them.

This view was exciting because it opened up a new panorama on the spirituality contained within the physical world, particularly in relation to certain aspects of biochemistry and physiology familiar to myself.

So the pages of this book have arisen mostly from talks given to Christian people in the Adelaide district many years ago. There always seems to be a few more insights/pearls which reveal themselves when one is asked to speak on this subject. As to whether this revelation is from God or not, only the reader can make that decision. However, my feeling is that the contents of this book are from God, as revealed by the Holy Spirit, because what is written concurs with God's word as expressed in the Bible. Secondly it is inconsistent with my usual way of thinking which is far more scientific than theological. My hope for this book is that the reader finds this revelation challenging, enlightening, lifegiving and uplifting. Anyway it is the Holy Spirit's job to convict the reader of this.

Why God may have motivated the writing of this book is a big question mark as it was never my intention to write a spiritual (or any) book for that matter. It cannot be because of my Christian walk as it is far from being as fervent or committed as it should be. To be honest, the author is an old cracked clay vessel but nonetheless still a work in progress for the Lord. On the positive side, Jesus Christ is my Lord and Saviour and, for those accepting him, salvation is through his sacrificial death on the cross of Calvary over 2,000 years ago. My experience, like many other Christians in this life, is that all blessings in this life and the next is through God's grace, love and mercy as expressed through His son Jesus Christ. Most Christians, like me, would agree that without God's grace and direction we'd have no chance of achieving anything worthwhile anytime, anywhere.

This book is written in a simple repetitive manner with much scientific jargon removed where possible, hopefully making it easily understood. Despite this simplification of science, an attempt has been made to be as accurate as possible without confusing the reader. Similarly, an attempt is made to present scriptural sayings as simply as possible but hopefully in a balanced way. May it reach the hearts, minds and souls of the people God may want to speak to through its pages.

A short biographical account of is given to allow the reader to assess my academic credentials in science. My birthplace was in Lucknow India in 1938, the eldest of five boys in our family. In 1948, we emigrated to South Australia where my parents sent me to both primary and secondary Catholic schools. After secondary school, work full-time as a laboratory analyst in the mining industry ensued whilst attending the University of Adelaide after hours in order to undertake a Bachelor of Science degree. After completing the degree, marriage to Denise followed in 1964 and we subsequently had three daughters and a son who unfortunately died stillborn in 1967. A position in the Department of Surgery at the University of Adelaide to set up a biochemistry research laboratory allowed me to fulfil a desire to do research in medical biochemistry. Whilst working full-time, I commenced a Master of Science programme in 1966. The research component of this degree entailed working on the mechanism of action of a clinical immunosuppressive drug called azathioprine which allowed clinical success in renal transplantation. Thanks to expert supervision by academic supervisors, the research went very well and a Doctor of Philosophy degree by Flinders University of South Australia was awarded in 1972. This was followed by a post-doctoral fellowship for 2 years in the cancer area and later a tenured position in clinical biochemistry in South Australian state government run laboratories.

My research publications have spanned a variety of diverse areas such as: cancer, immunodeficiencies, renal stone biochemistry, anti-inflammatory drugs, AIDS and the biochemical changes in psychological stress leading to impaired immunity . After about 75 research publications and 30 years experience as a Chief Medical Scientist in charge of a laboratory at Flinders Medical Centre retirement followed in 2003. My other work related responsibility was to teach medical students various aspects of medical biochemistry, immunology and haematology. For this activity, Senior Lecturer status was conferred on me by Flinders University of South Australia. Although retired there is still some teaching and research involvement in my life, in addition to writing this book.

My Christian training includes a Catholic school education as well as 4 years of experiences in various charismatic churches. On the 25th of July 1977, my Christian walk really took off following a personal touch from Christ after pray from a spirit-filled minister. That time saw a rededication of my life to Christ followed by an immediate life changing spiritual or born again transformation that only the Holy Spirit can effect in one's life. Prior to this life changing experience my Christian walk was practically non-existent. At that time, God, if he existed, was more of a strict school master living up there in Heaven just waiting for me to make a mistake. One could never seem to do enough to please him or experience his reality. In the end there was one spiritually worn out person who quit going to church and began to doubt whether God existed. Obviously, his love was not evident to me at that time. The following scripture in 1 Cor 2:14 described me to a tee: "But the natural man receiveth not the things of the spirit of God: for they are foolishness unto him: neither can he know them for they are spiritually discerned: that is discerned by the inner being of man." God however was very patient and it was the infilling of the Holy Spirit in early August 1977 which made his presence very real to me.

In about 1983, a Diploma by correspondence in Christian Studies with Vision College in Sydney, Australia was completed as a part time external student. In December 30th 1991, my wife Denise died of cancer. This was followed by marriage to my second wife Heather in June 1996 and by March 2002 we were divorced. The reason for the breakdown is complex suffice to say that it is difficult to bring two families together.

To the reader statements such as "revelation by the Holy Spirit", and "knowing Christ in a personal way" and others may seem superspiritual and heavy. Revelation by God is scriptual (Daniel 2:22,28,29; Amos 3:7; 2Tim 3:16; Eph 1:17; Rev 1:1) and is available to all Christians who are open to his leading. Revelation does not mean that God spends all his time talking to us. In fact the only time he spoke to me in 30 years as a Christian was when He spoke the words "Trust me". To me, revelation is when you have a deep conviction to do something or when something is a big mystery in your life then all of a sudden it seems clearer.

Let me give some examples. One Saturday morning in 1989, whilst lying in bed, this conviction to write this book came out the blue. There was also the conviction to call this book "The Physical Body: The Spiritual Body". There were no deep prophetic words in my ear, just an inner conviction deep within. There was also a revelation about evolution. This came about through my own background but by also listening to talks by others, both for and against evolution. At one moment in time evolution just seemed scientifically improbable. Most probably, my new found Christian walk caused certain doubts and questions to arise. As a new Christian there was initially a sense that evolution may have been God's plan for creation. Please do not shut off if you believe in evolution. Your belief in this area is fully respected. Salvation, does not hang on your belief or unbelief in evolution, but on the fact that Jesus Christ is your Lord and Saviour. Nonetheless some of my scientific colleagues do not believe in God because of their belief that evolution, not God, over many billions of years has resulted in all life forms on earth and the universe as we know it today. As such it is a very dangerous belief as it can close your mind to the possibility that God exists.

As you read, please be patient and try not to let your background, experiences and biases cause you to shut off what may seem unintelligible or theologically indigestible to you at this moment. Please question what seems hard to digest. The main aim of this book is to share my thoughts on this subject with you and perhaps give you a different point of view. Hopefully, this aim will be met by all who read these pages. It is not the intent of this book to change the basic structures of your beliefs. Only God can convince you to do that only if you need to.

Before concluding this section, just a short introduction is needed to define what is meant by the spiritual and physical body. Most of my concepts in this area have been borrowed from Christian teaching and to some extent common sense. Just as this book consists of physical and spiritual aspects of science, so is a person composed of both a physical and spiritual body. It is these two beings who make up the human being. The physical being is simply the body with all its very complex systems such the renal, brain, skeletal, hepatic, cardio-vascular, lymphatic, neuromuscular and many other systems. The physical being, as wonderfully created by God as it is, is here only for a short time and then dies because of sin.

The inner being or spirit is nondissectable and represents the eternal part of us (John 3:16; Gal 6:8). In fact the body without the spirit is dead (James 2:26). The spiritual being is the worshipful or intuitive part of us. It is that eternal part of us made in the image of God our creator (Gen 1:26) and in essence it is truly who we are. Therefore it represents everything positive and essentially good within us.

The further aspect of our being which is often mentioned in the literature is the soul. Though not absolutely clear on this, the spirit and soul are probably interchangeable terms. The spirit and the body can be polluted by sinful activities. In scripture there are many examples of people possessed by spiritual demons. This implies a spiritual pollution or Satanic powers influencing our minds and our spiritual life. In addition the physical side can be polluted by pollutants such as cigarette smoke, alcohol and drugs and other environmentally contaminating chemicals. This is discussed in more detail in the chapters to follow.

This book is not a treatise which knocks the physical part of us as being evil and bad. The physical body is an incredible wonder and reflects along with the rest of nature the wonderful, creative and artistic ability of God. God said of His creation, including us, that it was very good (Gen 1:31). Unfortunately because of our sin of disobedience in the Garden of Eden and our attempts to do our own thing apart from God, it became pollutable and eventually dies because of sin (Rom 5:12 and 8:10).

In this book the physical aspect of our being will be described first followed by an attempt to relate it to the spiritual aspect of our being. As indicated already, Christ is God who communicates with our inner being through the Holy Spirit and has much to do with its growth and full expression. Hence this book has much to say about Jesus Christ who to all Christians is God our creator and the source of our salvation (Eph 3:9; Col 1:16; Rev 4:11). My pray is that you receive much positive revelation, blessings and spiritual growth through reading its pages.

CHAPTER 2
GENES

Before launching into this complex section certain definitions need to be made mainly because science is a language all its own. Molecules are chemical substances such as methane (CH_4), carbon combined with hydrogen atoms. Sugar is another molecule with the formula $C_6H_{12}O_6$ comprising of carbon, hydrogen and oxygen atoms. Common salt ($NaCl$) is a molecule comprising of sodium and chlorine atoms. Polyvinyl chloride plastic or PVC comprises of many hundreds of molecules of vinyl chloride (CH_2CH-Cl) joined together chemically. Because it has many repeating units of vinyl chloride it is called a polymer.

Deoxyribonucleic acid or DNA is sometimes termed a polymer consisting of purine molecules (adenine, guanine, abbreviated A and G) and pyrimidine molecules (thymine and cytosine, abbreviated T and C) attached to a polymer of sugar called deoxyribose phosphate, hence the name deoxyribonucleic acid or DNA (most of it is located in the nucleus of the cell). A,G,C and T are termed bases because they contain nitrogen in their structure and are non-acidic. However the DNA structure overall is acidic because of the phosphate groups present in the molecule. Below I have likened the DNA to a string of 4 different coloured beads with the string being the deoxyribose sugar polymer and the beads the 4 bases of A,G,C,T.

Proteins, like DNA, consist of about 20 different amino acid molecules strung to gether. There is no sugar backbone as in DNA.

Their structure can be drawn aa1-aa2-aa3-aa4-aa5-etc (where aa = amino acid) and can be 1 to several thousand conjoined amino acids long. I have referred to the proteins as a string of beads of 20 different colours.

There is also another nucleic acid termed ribonucleic acid or RNA. It consists of a polymer of sugar ribose to which is attached the bases adenine, guanine, cytosine and uracil. It is important because bases in DNA codes for bases in RNA which codes for a specific amino acid sequence of a particular protein. Expanding on this, a group of 3 bases in DNA codes for a group of 3 bases in RNA and this group of 3 bases code for one specific amino acid. That is DNA codes for RNA which then codes for protein.The process of protein synthesis is more complex than this but there is no need to make it any more complex than this. In the discussion below I will repeat myself several times so that the process becomes more understandable. This is the most complex chapter to get across so please bear with me

Discussions relating to a biological knowledge of animals, including humans, sometime start at the molecules which code us, our so called blueprint molecules. These molecules are large polymers and are called by terms more or less equivalent to each other such as genes, nucleic acids, deoxyribonucleic acid or DNA and chromosomes. Genes consist of DNA and hundreds to thousands of genes make up one chromosome. There are 22 chromosome pairs, called autosomes (22 from Dad and 22 from Mum) in humans as well as the sex chromosomes X and Y which determines our sex; females have two X-chromosomes and males an X- and a Y-chromosome. Genes determine what we look like. For example our hair, eye and skin colour, our physical build, our overall general appearance. Our talents and personality are programmed genetically, although the environment also plays a significant contribution to the development of these traits.

Our genes are inherited from both parents and so we look more like one or other of our parents or, put differently, a mixture of them. Our complement of genes, inherited from our parents, were present in us when we were just a single cell in our Mother's uterus at the time of conception. This code is complex and it is basically determined by an arrangement of chemicals in our genes (that is it is a chemical code). Just as our thoughts and attitudes are expressed by speech or actions, our genes are expressed by the proteins they code for. For example gene A is a template or codes for protein A, gene B for protein B and so on. That is, genes determine the structure and therefore the function or activity of these proteins, which in turn determine our physical characteristics. Thus genes are the templates that make proteins which determine our physical characteristics.

The human genome has now been sequenced and each cell has been shown to contain about 30,000 genes or DNA tracts which code for about as many proteins. The incredible thing is that all this information is contained in a single cell, the ovum, about a millimeter in diameter. In this day and age of minaturization, it makes the most sophisticated computer look quite large and cumbersome.

Not all the genes in a cell are activily making protein all the time. For example, if one stops eating glucose for a few weeks, then the gene-derived proteins involved in metabolizing glucose will not be made because they are not needed. If we start eating glucose then these proteins will be turned on again. Similarly, if we fast by reducing our sugar intake, the body adapts to metabolizing fat stores more efficiently for energy requirements. It does this by making protein enzymes actively involved in fat metabolism. The brain is one tissue, for example, which starts to use fat metabolites for its energy usage instead of glucose, its normal source of energy.

In some cell types, certain genes/proteins are turned on or expressed whereas in other cells they are permanently turned off even though the genes for making these proteins are present in all cells of the body. For example, cells involved in fighting infection (called lymphocytes) activate their genes to produce antibody (a protein) to neutralize the infection. In contrast, muscle cells which are not involved directly in fighting infection have these antibody-forming genes except that they are permanently turned off and so muscle tissue rarely, if ever, make antibodies. Put differently, muscle cells do not make antibodies even though the genes for making them are present in these cells. So then every cell in the body only make those proteins related to its role in the body. Where those proteins are not required for the normal function of those cells then they are not made. This makes good sense - why make something when you don't need it or other specialised tissues are making it. In short there are genes which control other genes involved in protein synthesis. These control genes can turn on or off protein synthesis in certain cells.

In addition to the genes which code for proteins, there are great tracts of DNA which do not appear to have any function in that they do not code for proteins. These apparently useless or non-functional genes, often called junk genes, account for over 90% of the DNA in the cell. These bits of "junk" DNA which do not code for protein have recently been shown to have roles which are very likely to be important to the normal function of the cell. One analogy relating to the function of junk DNA is that it is like a dimmer switch on a lamp, the brighter the lamp the more protein is made and conversely the dimmer the light the less protein is made. So junk DNA ignored for many years and thought to be useless left over's from evolution is now known to have important control roles in cellular function. In time, it is very likely junk DNA will be shown to have many other important functions. So junk DNA is no longer termed so as it is being shown to be important for normal cell function.

The following paragraph is an attempt to chemically explain mutations. Mutate and change are interchangeable words. It is probably the most difficult area in this book for the lay person to comprehend and the scientist to simplify. Hopefully you will understand most of it. My apologies beforehand for not being able to simplify it enough.

Genes code for proteins and mutations are alterations to the normal gene structure or chemical code which results in changed or mutated protein products which generally do not function as well as their non-mutated or normal counterparts. Hence mutations are changes to the chemical message in the gene which results in a change to the protein coded by that gene. Hence DNA codes protein and mutated DNA codes mutated protein.

Proteins are large polymers of different size and function. On average they are about 1,000 amino acids long and require 3 times as many DNA bases of A,C,G,T (3,000) to code for it. Let us expand on this.

There are about 20 different amino acids found in any one protein and the sequence in which they occur in a protein determines the shape and function of that protein. Let's explain with a practical example.

A protein may be thought of as a necklace made up of 20 different coloured beads representing the 20 different amino acids. On average there is about 1,000 beads in this necklace. Depending on how you string these 20 differently coloured beads you will get many different necklaces - some with lots of blue, some with lots of red, gold, yellow etc. Your plans for designing this necklace determines the order of these beads just like DNA, the genetic plan, determines the order of the amino acids in the protein. So DNA dictates the order in which these beads or amino acids are strung together.

The chemical message in DNA is abbreviated by the following letters A, C, G and T. Each of these letters A, C, G, T represents a single chemical molecule of adenine, guanine cytosine, and thymidine respectively. The chemicals A, C, G, T are strung together, like beads, in a certain order to give the polymer DNA. In one human cell there are billions of these four chemicals coding for 30,000 gene products or proteins. As I said earlier, a typical protein consisting of 1,000 amino acids will require three-times this number of DNA chemicals, that is 3,000. In other words three different DNA chemicals of the four if you like (eg GCA) would code for one amino acid (for example a red bead) on the necklace. Likewise TGA which is different to GCA would code for another amino acid or blue bead.

Say for example a normal DNA code may have the sequence TAGCCTATGCGGTAA.. (normally they are much larger but for illustration have used a shortened version of DNA). With a mutation then the code may read as follows TAGC**G**TATGCGGTAA..(mutation

the physical body, the spiritual body

highlighted). In this mutation the fifth letter from the left, or chemical C, is now replaced by a different chemical, G which is shown in bold. Other mutations or changes may include the addition of an extra chemical (TAGCCTATTGCGGTAA...) or the loss of a chemical (TAGC. TATGCGGTAA...). All these alterations to the code are called mutations or, simply, changes to the normal code. That is the appearance of the DNA necklace is changed by removing or adding or replacing a bead to the necklace of DNA. This change of appearance is called a mutation and results in a change to the protein necklace since the protein structure is derived from DNA.

What happens when you have changes or mutations to DNA? If the protein is an enzyme then its enzymic activity can be unchanged, increased, decreased or removed altogether. In general, the latter two effects usually occur, that is the enzyme activity is reduced or deleted.

What effects can mutations to DNA have on us? They have deleterious effects on us. Usually the following spectrum of changes can occur with different mutations: mental retardation, blindness, deafness, cancer, inability to metabolise certain food constituents, inability to carry oxygen or distribute to tissues requiring it and many others. In general, mutations are not good because they have a damaging effect on us and are not good for us and not something that we would want. There is no such thing as a good mutation as they tend to reduce the quality and length of life. In textbooks on inherited diseases there are over 6,000 inherited mutations, none of them any good and result in either premature death or considerable morbidity.

How do we get mutations? They can be inherited from our parents. Fortunately most of our genes are duplicated with one copy coming from Dad and the other from Mum. If Dad is carrying a mutated or bad gene usually Mum's equivalent good gene compensates for it and vice versa. When both parents have a bad gene in the same place then this can be lethal or cause the baby to be born with a serious disease, for example like Cystic Fibrosis. The probability of this event occurring is increased when you have inter-marrying between close relatives since the probability of having two bad mutations on the same gene is greatly increased. Mutations can also occur during a process called meisosis when the parents to be are making eggs and sperm. For some unknown reason the DNA in these unfertilised cells have not sorted out themselves properly so that when conception takes place a mutation is present in the original embryo. Both of these mutations in the very early cell are called germ cell mutations. That is, they are there from the very beginning.

In contrast to the germ cell mutations where you inherit a bad DNA necklace, one can have somatic or acquired cell mutations where a good DNA necklace becomes damaged later on in life. That is, these mutations occur in mature cells and are acquired during life, usually after birth. These mutations are called somatic mutations.

So what causes mutations? Mutations usually occur when the cell is subjected to environmental pollutants such as is present in the air, food and water. Radiation either from the sun (ultra-violet), medical radiation (X-Rays) or from radioactive isotopes also causes mutations. We also generate, from normal metabolism, free radicals in our bodies. These radicals are normally neutralised by antioxidants but if in excess they can damage DNA. All these pollutants form a chemical bond with the chemical code or DNA base (with a DNA bead) present in good DNA (the whole DNA necklace) thereby causing it to be changed or mutated. These pollutants are chemicals such as 3,4-benzopyrene in cigarette smoke and other combustion products (industrial, car fumes), aflatoxins and nitrosoamines in food, metals such as chromium and nickel in the electroplating and similar related industries, asbestos and radium in the mining industries. Our most predominant free radicals generated from normal metabolism are superoxide anion and hydrogen peroxide. There are many antioxidants in our cells which can neutralize the damage caused by free radicals. Some of these, amongst many others, are such as ascorbate (vitamin C), vitamin E, vitamin A, coenzyme Q10 and glutathione.

It is probably true to say that most mutations are caused by pollution. For example, one of the most devastating effects of mutations is the formation of cancerous cells and the estimate by reputable cancer agencies is that up to 90% of cancers are caused by pollution. You are no doubt aware, for example, that cigarette smoking greatly increases the risk of lung cancer. Also Japanese who survived the atomic bombs dropped on their cities in World War 2 had a much greater incidence of blood related cancers such as leukaemia and lymphoma. Similarly those who survived the Chernobyl nuclear disaster will have an incresed tendency to form cancers. This is a very depressing scenario but we are all polluted and thereby mutated in our genes to a greater or lesser extent.

Though we live in a sea of pollution, especially those living in large industrial cities, we have developed a mechanism in our bodies of overcoming the effects of this pollution. We have in our cells enzymes which repair pollution damaged DNA. These are aptly referred to as DNA repair enzymes. There are several repair mechanisms operating in the cell to repair a variety of damages (eg. UV, X-Ray, chemical) to the DNA. Essentially what these enzymes do is to cut out the damaged part of DNA and replace it with good DNA. Persons who lack the ability to repair their DNA are very susceptible to cancer because the DNA, if unrepaired, inevitably results in a mutation and mutations have the potential to cause cancer. There is for example a clinical condition called Xeroderma Pigmentosa where the patients lack one repair enzyme used in repairing sunlight or UV radiation damage to DNA. These patients have to keep away from sunlight as they will develop multiple UV-induced skin cancers. Another effect of a deficiency of DNA repair in certain patients is that they age rapidly. This condition is known as Progeria, and these patients have a life span in their low teens. That is when they are teenagers they have the physical appearance and performance of someone about 60 - 70 years old. To sum up, mutations are not good as they cause many diseases like cancer, premature aging and many others.

In general, there is a better understanding now on how mutations cause cancer though the fine details are not fully known. It is known that we have in our chromosomes lengths of DNA which are known as protooncogenes. These genes are under strict control in the cell and are usually expressed in a controlled manner at certain times in the cell when they need to replicate or divide. Some protooncogenes act as growth factors and regulate the growth of the cell. Other genes called anti-oncogenes or tumour suppressor genes slow down cell division in order to permit DNA repair to occur and thereby reduce or inhibit the formation of mutations. If a mutation occurs in the DNA of protooncogenes or in anti-oncogenes they may become activated in the cell to produce certain proteins which inhibit normal controls for cell growth or indirectly DNA repair. When this happens mutations occur and the cell can turn into a cancer cell. Protooncogenes when activated are called oncogenes and as such can change a normal cell into a cancerous one. Similarly tumour suppressor genes if mutated can also cause the development of the cancer cell. In the normal human cell there are about a dozen protooncogenes, most of which if activated to an oncogene will generate cancers.

In addition to the several cancer producing genes (oncogenes) present in our cells, there are also viruses outside our bodies which have the ability to convert a normal healthy cell into a cancer cell. For example, there is a virus called HTLV-1 or Human T-cell Lymphotropic virus type-1. This virus, like others, is very small - about 1/100 the size of a normal cell. After entering the cell it inserts its genes into our genes. When it does this it replicates or reproduces making many copies of itself. Also, once inserted into our genes, this HTLV-1 virus causes our cells to turn into cancer cells by producing an imbalance of proteins in our cells which control cell division. Also certain types of human papilloma viruses (HPV) can cause cervical cancer. Recently a vaccine with antibodies active against HPV has been shown to prevent cervical cancer.

Another well known virus which also acts by a similar mechanism is called HIV-1 or Human Immunodeficiency Virus type-1. This virus is responsible for the disease called Acquired Immune Deficiency Syndrome or AIDS. HIV is attracted mostly to a particular white blood cell called the T-helper cell which has an active role in defending the body against invading organisms such as bacteria, viruses, foreign grafts and fungal infections. Once inside the cell, HIV inserts its genes into our genes. It then replicates itself by making many copies of itself so that it can infect many other cells similarly. This process of replication in the cell results in the death of T-helper cells involved in fighting infection, and so AIDS patients are at the mercy of the multitudes of disease-causing micro-organisms continually waiting to get at all of us in our environment.

The Bible has much to say about various family trees, especially the one relating to the family tree of Our Lord Jesus Christ. In Christ's family tree there were very many famous yet fallible people such as Adam, Seth, Noah, Abraham, Moses, Israel, David and many others. To my way of thinking, this chapter on genes has two important implications as far as the Bible is concerned, and these are considerations of evolution and salvation.

As a new Christian and staunch evolutionist, comments by well meaning Christians that evolution was against what the Bible said about creation made me feel uncomfortable. One tolerated these simplistic comments by saying that these people, as well meaning as they were, were not scientists and therefore did not understand the evolution story. To me, as a new Christian, evolution was viewed as God's plan for creating our world/universe. Nevertheless, one bore in mind that evolution is a theory and that it could possibly be wrong but until something better came along then one would stick by it.

To a scientist, a theory is a way of trying to explain an event or observation. For example one could have a theory that the unusual weather patterns that we observe now are due to atmospheric atomic bomb testing done years ago, or more recently, may be due to global warming.

A theory is different from a fact or a law. A law in science is something which is fact or proven indisputably by evidence or experimentation. For example the law of gravity states that we are attracted to the earth by a force equivalent to our mass or weight. We can easily prove the law of gravity by throwing a ball into the air; the law of gravity states the ball will come down because of its mass. There are many other laws. For example if we go through a red traffic light or speed, then the police will fine us for breaking the law of the road. The law is a definite fact which can be proven. Man made laws may be changed. For example a lawful right hand turn at an intersection last month may now not be permissible. Abortion was once illegal, whereas now it is legal. The natural laws are not so changeable. For example, one would not be so foolish to say that the law of gravity no longer exists unless apples stopped falling down off trees but fell up or just floated around.

Initially, the creation story seemed implausible and this in turn caused me discomfort, because deep down one knew that the Bible was inspired by the Holy Spirit and as such must be infallible and contain absolute truth. However, these unexplainable parts could be termed collectively as mysteries known only to God and taken on faith. Nonetheless, for me, two aspects of the Bible account of creation were difficult to reconcile. Firstly, how could the whole of mankind come from one man and one woman when it is a scientific fact that brother sister or close relative conception usually results in some sort of genetic deformity in the offspring? Secondly, how could man live to be nearly 1,000 years old? In the Genesis account many of the people near the early creation era lived well in excess of 900 years. This just did not ring true.

The rest of the creation account was digestible. God is God, and if He says that he created the world in 6 days, then he did. Though God is timeless, I believe that he uses time scales in the Bible that we can understand. That is his 6 days are 6 days and not 6 billion years. Like other creationists I now believe that God created the earth, universe and everything in it in 6 days some 6,500 years ago. If prehistoric animals came before us and died before the fall in the Garden of Eden this doesn't line up with God's word in Holy Scripture which states that death entered this world because of the sin of Adam (Rom 5:12; 8:10). That is before the fall, sin and death were not in existence in the animal kingdom. So how could early animals, including prehistoric mankind, die before the fall? Also when God created the earth and everything in it he said it was very good (Genesis 1:31). Death and suffering over millions of years are not really "very good".

Noah and the Ark was a scientifically plausible event as also was the flood. Jonah in the belly of the sea monster was also possible. However, relative intermarrying and absurdly high old ages were a bit hard to swallow until God's revelation kicked in. This revelation came from Dr Carl Wieland, of Creation Ministries International, at a grand round talk at Flinders Medical Centre in the 1990s. He opened my eyes and gave me an ah-ha moment. The explanation of it all goes back to the concept of the genes and mutations (changes to DNA) which had been staring at me in the face for many years.

When Adam and Eve were in the garden of Eden and fellowshipping with God, there was no such thing as mutations, disease, sin and consequently death in the animal kingdom. Man and woman were completely unpolluted living in harmony with God. God saw his creation and said that it was very good (Gen 1:31). Pollution, disease, sin and death, all not good events, were set into motion when man and woman disobeyed God and did their own thing (Rom 5:12, 8:10). Humans started to change physically and spiritually for the worse from that time on. When they were cast off from the garden, their genes were still intact with zero mutations present in them. Thus brother sister conception was scientifically feasible (low mutation rates) without the attendant genetic consequences we have nowdays. However, when the level of mutations had risen, through the passage of time, to an unacceptable level, God then forbade close relatives intermarrying (Lev 18:6-17). Also as mutations were accumulating in the genes of humans over a period of time we see that, in the bible account, the age of humans starts to decrease gradually (Gen 5:3-32; 11:10-25). Modern medicine has resulted in some prolongation in the lifespan since the 1950s but that is only a slight upward kink in longevity due to better nutrition, importance of exercise, new medicines such as antibiotics and vaccinations and in general better clinical care.

As indicated, once the mutation frequency increases, the age span decreases and this was shown earlier to occur dramatically in patients with an accelerated aging disease called Progeria. This revelation helped me understand in a satisfactory way the longevity and the close relative intermarrying which must have occurred in the creation/ genesis account in the Bible.

The theories on the foundation of the earth/universe, to me, has two major flaws which go against the two basic laws of thermodynamics. Note use of the term "laws". The first law of thermodynamics states that energy cannot be created or destroyed, but may be changed from one form to another. Putting it simply, you never get something from nothing. That means that one cannot make a lump of wood from thin air. A magician can, but you know that that lump of wood was in existence before - he was just hiding it from us. Similarly, that lump of wood cannot disappear as though it never existed. Sure, it can be burnt and converted it into light, heat and chemical (carbon dioxide, ash residue) energy but it cannot just disappear as though it never existed.

This earth and the universe that surrounds us is matter just like that lump of wood. The first law of thermodynamics says that it could not come into existence out of nothing. So where did our universe with its 96 stable elements come from - it sure is a lot of matter. Only God is able to create something like a small block of wood or this massive universe out of nothing. Scientists can say it arose from a big bang (if you are a big bang theorist). If the big bang is a fact then where did the matter/elements come from for the big bang to do its work? Science cannot explain the existence of matter from nothing because it goes against the first law of thermodynamics. Matter, therefore, points toward the existence of God, an originator, a creator (Gen 1; Coll 1:16,17).

The second law of thermodynamics states that matter is in a state of increasing entropy. All this means is that everything is wearing out, breaking down, running out of useful energy. We all know for example that things like cars, lawn mowers, clothes and ourselves for that matter are wearing out. Evolution states that man has evolved from primordial soup in an upward way in contravention of the second law.

According to evolution, the atmosphere of this planet was once a mass of gases (where did they come from?) which under electrical activity in the atmosphere caused these molecule gases to join together to form more complex molecules. These complex molecules then formed the complex biological molecules as we know them today. These molecules then started to reproduce themselves leading to the formation of the most primitive unicellular organism. This simple organism under changing environmental conditions involving mutations and natural selection then went on to form more complex organisms. This process then continued on and on over many billions of years until eventually you arrived at the human being, the pinnacle of evolution at this point in time. All this goes against the second law because it goes from larger entropy (gases) to greater organisation or smaller entropy (humans). Also gases under an electric discharge or any other input do not form the life chemicals in our cells. And even if they could form these chemicals they could never organize themselves into a simple cell. It is a bit like saying hurricanes going through a metal yard for billions of years could result in a Boeing 747 or an computer. The human cell has far more design and complexity than these man made/designed devices. Also 747s and PCs cannot reproduce themselves, unlike a cell.

As a Biochemist the molecules that make up life are of interest. The molecules in humans are so complex and each molecule depends on the other for its existence. As already indicated, you cannot have even a minor departure from molecular structure (mutation) without things going bad. For example DNA makes another nucleic acid called ribonucleic acid or RNA. There are many different forms of RNA like ribosomal, messenger and transfer RNA . These basic messenger RNAs can have up to 30,000 types which code for just as many proteins. The DNA is a huge polymer with a particular chemical sequence for each protein they code for. RNA also is a polymer made off these huge DNA polymer templates. The DNA code in humans is 3 billion bases long. If 3 million of these code for our proteins then the probability of these bases being strung together in the right sequence for life is therefore $1/4^{3 \text{ million}}$. A rather small number,in fact an impossibility.

As indicated earlier in this chapter proteins are also huge polymers made off the DNA and RNA templates. Proteins are made up of 20 different amino acids, each of which must follow a particular structure, otherwise nothing will work in the cell. Some proteins convert DNA into DNA for cell replication. Some other proteins convert DNA into RNA and some proteins use RNA to make other proteins. Some proteins in the cell have a role in maintaining the structure of the cell. Other proteins are involved in preventing certain bits of DNA from being converted into RNA. Conversely, other proteins allow bits of DNA to be converted into RNA. Many proteins in the cell are involved in generating energy for the cell. As you can see the cell is incredibly complex with each molecule interdependant on the others. Every one of the tens of thousands of proteins in the cell is dependent on every other protein in the cell and must have the right structure, otherwise nothing will work and the cell will die. The machinery of the cell is so complex and balanced that humans, after spending billions of research dollars, have a basic understanding on how the cell works. In short, there is incredible design and balance in the cell and only God could design anything so complex. To say that it just came into being by chance is the height of improbability, in fact impossible. It also is a terrible insult to God our creator.

Did the protein evolve first, then the DNA, or what? This is an important question because every molecule in the cell is in significant relationship to every other molecule. There is a molecular symbiosis in the cell just as there is a plant/animal/insect symbiosis in our planet. You all know how tightly balanced our environment is. If you cut down forests then you upset the animal, insect and atmospheric ecology of the earth. There is a tightly balanced interrelationship between animals, plants and insects. You destroy one of these, then you upset the whole ecology. Similarly in the cell, there is an symbiosis between all the molecules in the cell. You destroy a few of these or even change one and you throw the whole system out of equilibrium.

Evolution would have that these molecules were floating about and through the passage of time, whammo, they all came together and it all worked and life was born or initiated. Supposing that did happen, then where did all the cellular membranes that hold all the molecules together come from? To go from one animal form (ape) to another (human) requires huge mutational changes. As indicated even slight mutational changes usually spell disaster. As you can see, evolution is just so improbable that it is impossible. Only God could orchestrate anything as complex as a cell. As mentioned, a computer is in no way as complex as the cell, but to say that it just evolved from a whole pile of minerals lying around the place is more probable than to say that the cell just happened this way through chance.

Evolution would have that early humans came about 1-2 million years ago and humans as we know them today (Homo Sapiens) arrived on the scene 100,000 to 200,000 years ago. From biblical genelogy we were created by God about 6,500 years ago with death and suffering arriving in the Garden of Eden at about this time resulting from Adam and Eve's disobedience. If biblical creation is all pie in the sky then why did Jesus Christ himself state "But from the beginning of creation, God made them male and female" (Mark 10:6). Also in Luke 11:50-51 Jesus said "That the blood of prophets which was shed from the foundation of the world may be required of this generation. From the blood of Abel to the blood of Zacharias...". This shows from the very words of Jesus that humankind was present from the beginning of creation not million or billions of years later. So this is very significant because Jesus is God and cannot err. Even as a human he was truly God and truly man (Phillipians 2:6-7). He emptied himself by becoming man but he was still fully God. It is similar to me when I play with my young grandkids and kids. I would sometimes get on all fours and make out I was a horse, lion or dog and chase them but at the same time I was still a scientist. The concepts of a new earth (Rev 21 and 22), Resurrection (1 Cor 15), atonement (Romans 5:12-21) all hinge on a proper understanding of the first few chapters of Genesis, that is on biblical history. If you do not believe the first few chapters of Genesis then why should the rest of the bible be believable? Also if you want to delve at greater depth into the creation/evolution issue go into the link creation.com.

The other aspect of genes which relates to the word of God is the teaching on salvation. In John's Gospel chapter 3 Jesus was talking with Nicodemous, a highly respected priest of the religious sect called the Pharisees. Jesus said to Nicodemous that he had to be born again in order to enter Heaven (John 3:3). Nicodemous appeared to be confused by this term "born again". It is a term which is frequently used by many Christians and one which can cause confusion. As one would have expected, Nicodemous argued with Jesus about how could he get back into his mother's womb and be born again (John 3). Physically it is an impossibility.

The understanding about being born again came to me one day unexpectedly. In our earthly conception, the genes of our mother and father come together in the sperm and egg and combine to form one cell, namely us. This single cell has all the information about our myriad characteristics such as height, eye colour, skin texture and so on. All these characteristics are a mixture of the genes of our mum and dad. Hence, we have dad's big nose, mum's blue eyes, and so on. In other words, we look like our parents. Similarly when we are spiritually conceived or born again, the spiritual genes of Jesus Christ and our spiritual genes come together in this second birth. Once this happens the things of God start to make sense whereas before they were foolishness. We now start to see things through God's eyes. The Bible, once a boring book now becomes alive.

We develop the spiritual characteristics of God just like at conception we received our genetic material and developed the physical characteristics of our parents. The exciting thing about this event is that it occurs so simply. It is simply a decision by us to admit to our sinfulness to God, repent from past sins, reject Satan and all his works and ask Christ to be our Lord and Saviour and take over the reins of our life. Perhaps the classical physical yet spiritual example of this event happening occurred when Mary conceived of Jesus by the

Holy Spirit when she said "Yes" to God (Luke 1:38). In the same sense we are conceived by the Holy Spirit when we also say "Yes" to Jesus and are transformed by God's spiritual genes, by Christ living within us (Gal 2:20). That is Christ's Spirit and our spirit or inner being meld into one - Christ in us and us in Christ (Gal 2:20, 3:28; 1 John 4:12-16; Rom 8:10, 16:7;).

Another analogy came to me one day. The Cross with Christ on it is like the sperm which penetrated the earth (egg) on Calvary's hill nearly 2,000 years ago and brought this earth back to life. Christ's death like the sperm's demise allowed us (the ovum) to live on eternally in happiness and joy with our Saviour. Christ's genes and our genes come together in our spiritual hearts and as a result we start to express the Christ nature when we become born again. The expression of Christ's genes within us becomes more and more manifest as we feed His genes by hearing and obeying the word of God. This is just like the natural genes for synthesizing sugar become turned on as we eat more and more sugar.

Being sensitive to the Holy Spirit of God allows further expression of the Christ life within us because we get more revelation of the beauty of who Christ is. If, however, we disobey God and continue in sin after accepting Christ into our lives as Lord and Saviour, this Christ life within us is stifled and cannot grow, and the sin genes are further activated (John 5:14; Rom 6; 1,2; 1 John 3:8-10; 5:16-18). One could say that Judas was an example of the latter situation. His greed for money and power broke down his fidelity to God and he betrayed Jesus.

This activation of the sin gene is like turning on the cancer gene or oncogene mentioned earlier. Expression of the oncogene is a physical counterpart of the spiritual counterpart sin. One results in cancer (physical death) the other in spiritual death. Christ's genes within us are like anti-oncogenes or tumor suppressor genes. They turn off the sin gene or better still prevent its formation if we allow his power to work through us (cf Rom 7:14-25 to Rom 8:1-17; 1 John 3:7-10, 4:12). No wonder Paul says that we must reckon ourselves dead to sin (Rom 6:2,11; 1 John 3:6; 1 Peter 2:24; 2 Cor 5:17). That is, the oncogene or sin gene equivalent in our lives is turned off or dead if one belongs to Christ. With the help of the Holy Spirit we can turn off this sin or "spiritually equivalent" oncogene. On becoming a Christian the sin gene doesn't get removed unfortunately and tries, as you well know, to reactivate itself, just like the oncogene, to the day we die. However with God's help, through the Holy Spirit, we can keep it silent. Without God's help we have no chance of resisting sin.

This closeness that God requires of us in our relationship with him is emphasized often in the Bible. For example many times we are called the children of God which implies a genetic linkage (Rom 8:16-21; 9:26; Gal 3:26-29; 1 John 3:9,10; John 11:52; Matt 5:9). In one epistle, Paul says it is no longer he who lives, but Christ living within him (Gal 2:20). Christ said that we are the branches and He is the vine, and He talks of us being grafted in (John 15:1-5). In order for this to happen there must be genetic compatibility between Our Lord and ourselves. You cannot graft a thorn bush with an apple tree. The Bible also talks of us having the mark or seal of God on us (Eph 1:13; 4:30; 2 Cor 1:22; 2 Tim 2:19; Rev 9:4). This is akin if you like to us looking like our parents. Their mark is on us. Jesus also hinted of our closeness with Him when He said eat my body and drink my blood (John 6:53; Mark 14:22-24; Matt 26:26-28). Christians at communion time re-enact symbolically this oneness with Christ by eating and drinking of Christ's body and blood. Also we the Church are called the bride of Christ (Rev 21:2,9; Eph 5: 23-33), once again emphasizing our spiritual oneness or union with Him.

In all this discussion, it must be stressed that it is Christ alone who has done it all for us and given us His life for and within us. All that He asks is that we acknowledge our sinfulness, give our lives to him and accept Him as Our Lord and Saviour (John 3:16-19). It is a simple decision but one with eternal consequences. God's only motive for doing this for us is His deep and abiding love for us.

The Bible says that all our righteousness is like dirty rags and all have fallen short of the Glory of God (Isa 64:6; Rom 3:23). In other words we may be good guys and help those around us. The world may hold us up as an example of goodness but it is never enough to get us to Heaven because our goodness lags light years behind God's requirements. It is the precious blood of Our Lord Jesus Christ which washes away our sins, reconciles us to God and gives us the righteousness of Christ (Rom 5:9; Eph 1:7;2:13; Heb 9:11-14; 1 John 1:7; Rev 1:5; 5:9; 7:14). It is His precious blood which gives us meaningful life down here as well as allowing us the reward of eternal life after we die . Jesus said He has come that we may have life and have it more abundantly (John 10:10). People blame Our Lord for all the heartache, sickness and tragedy in our lives. But it was us who turned away from him in the garden of Eden and we are still paying the price for this disobedience. On many occasions when the chips have been down it may feel like God doesn't love us. Anyway it is unlikely for God to harm us because God is love and gave his life for us. Yes thank God for his patience, forgiveness, mercy, love and the righteousness of Christ imparted to us mainly through what Christ has done (Rom 3:22;4:6,11; 8:10; 1 Cor 1:30, Phil 3:9).

It is not for us to judge others, heaven forbid. God the Creator has blessed us greatly in His creation. Life without Christ loses its excitement. Christ adds that abundance to our lives that he mentions in John 10:10. Not in monetary or earthly riches but in that deep peace of soul which the material things can never give (John 14:27; Phil 4:7; Eph 2:14). The fact of the matter is that Jesus is the giver of life to all who come to Him and accept His plan of salvation. It is our deeply personal relationship with Our heavenly Father (once again the spiritual/genetic link) which is most important. Sure, we hear of Christians killing Christians, but those people will some day have to give an account of their murder to Almighty God. We must work at our own salvation (Phil 2:12) and cultivate those genes of Christ within us. What any other Christians do is between them and God. Obviously, if they are disobeying the word of God then we must in love and much wisdom correct and counsel them being mindful to pray for them and ourselves as well that we do not also stray.

To conclude this section on genes, it must be emphasized again that it is God who gives us an eternal life in Heaven through His Son

Jesus Christ. When we die our spirits live on either eternally in torment or eternally in peace and happiness with Our Lord and Saviour Jesus Christ. This joyous eternal life is a free, wonderful and glorious gift from Almighty God just like the physical life that we enjoy is a free gift from God through our parent's union. By the grace of God we have salvation. We have a physical birth through our parents union and a spiritual birth through our union with Christ. This Christian life that we are blessed with is a close unity or oneness with our Heavenly Father. It is Christ's genes within us which have blessed us not only in this short life on earth, but also eternally in the next life in heaven. When we look on our children we can see our characteristics in them. Similarly, when Almighty God looks upon us He sees His Son Jesus Christ in us because of what Jesus did at Calvary 2,000 years ago. Just as the Father and Son are one so also are we in Christ. What a wonderful gift we have within us, the genes of Almighty God through His Son Jesus Christ. To Christians this unity with Christ, the Holy Spirit and God our Father is the essence of the wonder and excitement of being a Christian. It gives balance to our lives on earth not to mention the reward of eternal existence and fellowship with God Our Father. And the gift is free. All we have to say is yes to Jesus Christ. Any life including the Christian life is not an easy one but with God's help as Christians we have a peace down here despite all the hassles. Like many others having lived both lives Christians know which is the best one by far. God's yoke is much easy to carry than the one the world or Satan puts on us. All praise and glory to Jesus Christ for His love, grace and mercy toward us. He is a wonderful God and the source of all that is good in this life.

CHAPTER 3

THE SIGNICANCE OF BLOOD

Someone once said to me that there appears to be a thread of blood running through the books of the Bible. For example, God was pleased with Abel's blood sacrifice and displeased with the Cain's sacrifice of wheat (Gen 4:11-16). Later we read of God's command to sprinkle animal's blood on the altar of God to expiate the sins of the people (Ex 12: 13; 24:6-8; 29: 16,20). In the New Testament we witness the fulfillment of that earlier blood sacrifice for sin when Christ himself became our sacrificial lamb and died on the Cross of Calvary for our sins (Eph 1: 7; 2: 13; Coll 1: 14, 20; Heb 9: 12-14; 1 Peter 1: 2,18,19; Rev 1: 5). Scripture reminds us that the life is in the blood (Deut 12: 23). In this section both the physical and spiritual significance of blood will be compared.

Blood consists of a pale yellow liquid called plasma in which the red and white blood cells are suspended. The white blood cells are involved in neutralizing foreign or hostile invaders of the body such as viruses, bacteria and cancer. The red blood cell, abbreviated RBC, predominant in blood being 1,000-fold higher in numbers than the white blood cells. It is these RBCs that give blood its characteristic dark red colour. The discussion will centre initially on RBCs and then white blood cells later.

RBCs are derived from a cell in bone marrow called a stem cell. Bone marrow stem cells have the potential to develop or change into 3 different functional cell groups in blood. They can become infection fighting white blood cells (neutrophils, monocytes, lymphocytes) or cells involved in preventing blood loss (platelets) or RBCs. A hormone, erythropoeitin, produced mainly by the kidney, directs the stem cells in bone marrow to divide and change into RBCs. One stem cell gives 16 fully developped RBCs in about 5-7 days. Once formed, the RBC is released from the bone marrow to do its functions in the blood stream.

To generate RBCs the stem cell has to undergo four rounds of cell division or replication over the period of about a week. With each replication cycle or cell division, the resulting daughter cells becomes progressively smaller and smaller. Eventually the cell looses its nucleus which is a critical part of the cell because it contains the genetic or coding information which is important to normal cell function (see Chapter on Genes). The RBC is therefore unique in that it lacks genes and one would expect it not to live long. However, despite being deprived of its DNA, the essential component or blueprint of life, the RBC goes onto survive 120 days. It is also the most mobile of all cells of the body travelling something like 2.5 Km/day or 300 Km during the course of its lifetime. Not bad for a cell 1/100 mm in diameter.

So what does a red cell look like? It has a doughnut-like shape, often described as a biconcave disc. With this shape the RBC can fold in on itself, like a hinged table top, allowing it to get through gaps which are 3-fold smaller in diameter than itself. This property allows the cell to get into areas that it would normally not be able to if it were not flexible.

What does the RBC do? Its main function is to carry oxygen, the life giving gas, and distribute it in its travels to all the various tissues of the body. It is obviously true therefore that the life (in the form of oxygen) is in the blood (Deut 12: 23). Even though every tissue/cell contributes to the well being of every other tissue/cell and is essential to the overall working of the body, it is blood which gives life/oxygen to every one of these tissues. The RBCs are not completely autonomous in this function in that the heart is needed to pump these cells around the body and the lungs to fill them up with oxygen and at the same time remove excess carbon dioxide from them. Normally, the lungs are inflated with oxygen-containing air however when lung function is impaired by asthma, emphysema or lung cancer then oxygen transfer to the RBCs is impaired and the entire body suffers and becomes tired easily because of oxygen deprivation.

Within the RBC, oxygen is carried by a red coloured molecule called haemoglobin. Haemoglobin consists of an iron containing molecule called haem which in turn is slotted into a large protein molecule called globin. Globin can be likened to a bread roll with the haem molecule inserted into the roll like a slice of beef. Hence the red coloured molecule in RBCs consists of four haem molecules (or beef slices) in four attached globin molecules (attached bread rolls). Although it is the iron atom in haem (beef slice) which binds strongly to oxygen, the globin (bread roll) helps in this process.

In humans there over 200 different mutations reported for haemoglobin. The mutations occur in the globin molecule resulting in an alteration of its normal bread roll shape. Some globin mutations result in haemoglobin binding oxygen too tightly thereby depriving tissues of it. In contrast, other mutations result in oxygen being bound too loosely so that it is lost before it gets to the tissues. Generally cells with mutated haemoglobins do not live very long and are destroyed by other cells in the body. This results in anaemia or low blood haemoglobin concentrations in patients with these mutations.

Oxygen is released by the RBCs and absorbed by outlying tissues of the body where it does the job of generating the energy molecule of the cell adenosine 5-triphosphate or ATP as it is abbreviated (discussed further in the chapter on the gasses of life and death). Oxygen does this by interacting with the products of food metabolism, namely protein, glucose and fat. This biochemical process, termed oxidative phosphorylation, is complex and generates the much needed energy-giving molecule of the cell, ATP. Without food you eventually run out of energy (ATP) and die. Another chapter on nutrition discusses the medical consequences of not efficiently absorbing glucose, fat and other molecules into the cells.

To help release oxygen at tissues, RBCs makes a molecule called 2,3-diphosphoglycerate or DPG. DPG by binding to haemoglobin facilitates the release of oxygen from RBCs to the tissues. Without DPG the tissues would be deprived of oxygen and work sub-optimally because of a lack of energy.

To recap, the RBC is a flexible cell which is unique in that it has no genetic material yet lives 120 days, travels many times around the body and does a very important task in transporting the life giving gas oxygen and donating it to all the tissues of the body.

To me, oxygen is the physical analogy or equivalent to the word of God. Jesus once said "the words that I have spoken to you are spirit and are life" (John 6:63). Peter realized this when he said to Jesus "You have the words of eternal life" (John 6:68). Oxygen therefore, if you like, is spiritual in that it cannot be seen and also it is life giving to the physical body by helping generate ATP the energy giving molecule so essential to the life of the cell. The word of God can be seen in written form but, in its spiritual, invisible form, it is eternally life giving to our spirits and how it does this is an aspect which is a mystery to us. All I know is that reading God's word or biblical holy scripture enlivens me spiritually and this is the testimony of many Christians I have met.

The process of the RBC formation is symbolic of Christian growth and development. The haemoglobin in the RBC represents spiritually the Holy Ghost or Holy Spirit, the third person of the Divine Trinity, within us. The word of God states that it is the Holy Spirit who teaches and enlivens the word of God to us (1 Cor 2: 12-16). As the stem cell in the bone marrow on its way to becoming a RBC, looses more and more of its precious genetic material and becomes smaller and smaller physically in becoming a RBC so it gains more and more haemoglobin. That is the two components, loss of genes/size and gain of haemoglobin are inversely proportional. As the genetic material decreases so the haemoglobin concentration of the cell increases. In our own walk in life as we let go of or lose more and more of what we once considered important to life, so God is able to fill us more and more with the Holy Spirit. The more we have of the Holy Spirit in our lives the more effective will our role be because firstly we will understand more fully the word of God and secondly we will be able to carry more of the word of God and distribute it more effectively to others in need, just as the RBCs distribute oxygen. The essence of this word is Jesus Christ (the word made flesh) and by understanding more of Him (His goodness, grace and love) in our lives so will we be empowered to give more of this life giving word to others around us (Coll 1: 9-11; Phil 4: 13; Eph 3: 16-21). By giving the life giving word of God may not necessarily mean preaching although that may be how God will use you. Your attitude of Christ-like love will speak more highly than a thousand sermons. If people want Christ they must want Him because they can see Him in you. In fact, our lives may be the only glimpse of the Gospel that our friends and colleagues may ever see.

All Christians are in ministry in one form or another. The molecule, DPG, represents our attitude or disposition. Are we givers or takers? Do we have God's word, talents, finance, abilities and hold onto them or do we distribute them with a loving and willing heart to those in greater need than ourselves? For it is only by giving that we can be filled up again (Luke 6: 38). Similarly RBCs depleted of oxygen are refilled with this life-giving gas in the lungs.

You do not have to be a pastor or priest or a missionary to be in ministry. Once you invite Christ into your lives then you are empowered by God to become a child of God. In fact we are referred to as a royal priesthood (1 Peter 2:9). When God is dealing with us it can be a very painful process in recognising and giving up things and attitudes which are, over years, ingrained and precious to us. God however replaces our worldly losses and negative attitudes with His presence more and more in our lives. So we really gain spiritually though many times we feel that we are hard done by, perhaps because to the world we are pitiful, dumb, poor or unsuccessful. One professor colleague called me a Jesus freak and I wore that title with pride and honour. Besides I would much rather be a Jesus freak than a Satan freak. The RBC becomes progressively smaller as it develops and in the world's eyes, in many respects, we become smaller as we embrace Christ more and more and our aims and aspirations change direction. To many in the world, success is probably gauged by academic achievements, the size of your bank balance/investments or other material accumulations such as how large your house/car/boat is. But it is a fairly pitiful scale for measuring success. You are successful because you are made in the image of God and therefore have the potential and goodness of God within you (Gen 1).

As Christians, our hope and prayer is that the image of God becomes progressively imprinted on us as we walk daily with Him. One day, the Bible says that we will be transformed into the likeness of Jesus as we come before Him (1 John 3: 2; Phil 3: 20,21). You cannot get any more successful than that, can you? This worldly success is like a wisp of vapour which lasts for only a very short season. The success of being in Christ has significant eternal ramifications and it also has a deep and everlasting peace associated with it (even down here) which is not circumstance dependant. So if things are tough hang on and pray and praise God more because Jesus wants to see your faith and trust in Him grow. Regardless of the circumstances, when you are in Christ you are always successful because when God looks at you He sees His Son. Besides, Jesus has gained us the victory over the devil, death and the world about 2,000 years ago. So we come from a position of victory regardless how we feel or what we may be going through (Rom 8:35-39; 1 John 5: 4,5).

Worldly success is a noble aim and not an unworthy aspiration. God wants us to succeed in being a good business man, plumber, carpenter, teacher, scientist or whatever. When people see your conscientious Christ-like attitude, this is a great testimony to God and success will inevitably follow. However, when we focus solely on success and thereby relegate God to second place or lower, then things get out of balance. Our prosperity should be in Christ and not the trinkets of this world no matter how alluring they may be. As the Bible says "But seek for His kingdom, and these things shall be added unto you" (Luke 12: 31). In other words give God top priority and centre stage in your life and everything else will fall into place.

The other interesting aspect of blood, is the union of oxygen with the iron in the haem molecule. Scripture describes the Word of God as being a double edged sword (Heb 4:12; Rev 1: 16). That is it is like an iron weapon. The Word also says this weapon will penetrate down deep to where the bone and marrow meet (Heb 4:12). That is the Word of God will go down to the innermost parts of our being and cut out those negative attitudes which God would remove for our well being, healing and growth into Him. Growth is a painful process - just think back on your early teens. But from this growth in Christ, comes increasing strength, joy, healing and peace.

Even though the word of God is like a sword, God does not want us to use His Word/sword to attack others whose lives we perceive do not match up. There is not much love in that. Scripture says to remove first the log or wrongful attitudes from our own lives (Luke 6: 42) with the iron of His word. This is not a request to self-flagellate. We are told to love our neighbour as ourselves (Mark 12: 31 - 33). Therefore do not condemn yourself or anyone else, God will convict you or them of any failings if He needs to. We are commanded to love and not judge as love is the major key to a successful Christian life. As Christians (RBC equivalents) we need to move ego (DNA) more and more out of our lives. That way more of the Holy Spirit (haemoglobin) can move in our lives and we can become more useful for God in our ministering to others.

Another interesting aspect of the RBC is that after giving oxygen to the tissues it receives from these tissues an end product of metabolism, a gas called carbon dioxide. As indicated in greater detail in the chapter on gasses, an increase in carbon dioxide in the body will cause acidosis. That is the body becomes acidic. The RBC with water converts this carbon dioxide to a substance called bicarbonate which neutralizes acidity. Also, haemoglobin binds the acid part and neutralizes it thereby allowing the cells of the body to function. The red blood cell releases this acid in the lungs by reconverting it to carbon dioxide which is then blown out by the lungs into the atmosphere. So the RBC beside feeding the tissues with oxygen is also involved in getting rid of acids which are life threatening if not dealt with. As Christians we need to help release any bitterness (acids) within us and others. With the help of the Holy Spirit (haemoglobin), human bitterness can be neutralized and released. As physical acidity in humans can destroy or inhibit normal, healthy physiological functions so this bitterness/unforgiveness in us can inhibit the full development of our human and spiritual potential.

The mutated haemoglobins discussed earlier are like Christians who do not have the true spirit of God. Some may hold onto the word so tightly to the exclusion of others who may need to hear the word. Or, more importantly, they may withhold love where it is needed. It is important not only to hold onto the word tightly but also to feed those in need of that word, love and support as the need arises. God promises that He will replenish us as we give (Luke 6:38). As with other mutated haemoglobins, some use the word too freely and throw it around anywhere and everywhere, mostly to condemn others. For example when someone is in distress they may say "As you sow so shall you reap" which though it is scriptual (Gal 6: 7) should not be used to condemn those already under stress. Jobs friends in the Bible were a bit like that in telling him his suffering was due to unrepented sin.

The other mutated spirit is the relegous spirit which says things like "Our Church is the true one" or "We have more light than other Churches" or "Unless you speak in tongues then you are not saved" or "Blood transfusions are sinful and opposed by God". That is these spirits take the word of God out of context and impose their biases on other people causing them to come under condemnation. There is nothing new. Satan used God's holy scripture to try and trip up Jesus who is the fleshly representation of the word of God. Jesus had been fasting 40 days and was feeling weak when Satan tried to tempt Him with God's word taken out of context (Matthew 4:1-11). But Jesus rebuked him by putting in the correct and true meaning of scripture. This was in contrast to Adam and Eve who were conned by Satan using the word of God cunningly yet incorrectly (Gen 3:1-6). Jesus was also hassled by the Pharasees and Saducees who tried many times to trip

Him up using scripture incorrectly (Mark 2:223-28; Matthew 22:23-46). They had no success and because of their jealousy and frustration had Him crucified on a cross. It is interesting that Jesus got very angry with those self righteous people who used the Word against others but who themselves did not live up to the requirements or essence of Holy Scripture but instead put on a pretence of self-righteousness and holiness (Matthew 23:1-39). As Christians, we need to be on guard to walk the talk rather than talk the walk like the Pharasees. Action speaks louder than words.

The other area where the word is mutated or changed relates to messages Christians get from God. They come out with statements like "The Lord has shown me that you have a spirit of unforgiveness or lust or whatever". These comments are generally untruthful, are ascribed to God and have a devasting effect on people they are aimed at. For example a person in one Church wanted me to pray that God would deliver her from a demon that was causing her to be a manic depressive. She was so relieved that her condition was not directly demonic and I then gave her a short course at the altar on what biochemically causes manic depression. After we agreed and prayed for her healing in Christ. The whole Church had labelled her as having a demon which one day would be got rid of and her condition would immediately be resolved. Not a nice label to have carry around - the woman with the demon.

Another Christian man went around in shame because his wife said that he had a spirit of lust. He went to every top reputable deliverance ministry in town for help. They all discerned he was spiritually OK. He was not a womaniser and was a faithful Christian husband. But for 5 years he carried this stigma put upon him by his Christian wife.

It is a very dangerous thing to ascribe words to our Lord which you imagined he spoke to you or to take His word out of context. Like cells with the mutated haemoglobin you could have a short life span. Using God's name or His word out of context is taking the name of the Lord God in vain. That is right, it is against His commandments and God said that He will not leave anyone unpunished who takes His name in vain (Exodus 20:7). Words from God should edify the Church and build up the person. So if you are judging or pulling down a fellow human in God's name be very careful. You could be inhibiting the growth of a human soul as well as your own by using God's message unwisely. Therefore use Holy Scripture with much pray and be sure that it is Holy Spirit directed. We do not want a mutant or Satanic spirit to stuff up people's lives.

To conclude the RBC represents a model of what a Christian should be to their community. This Christian gives out life by being a manifestation of Christ to the community. They will, like the RBC, be servers, comforting and nuturing those with hurts and thereby allowing them to release those hurts and be healed through an example of the Christ like love within us.

The other cellular component of blood is the white blood cell fraction. These cells are involved in fighting infection and foreign invaders to the body including cancer. They are also formed in the bone marrow from stem cells similar to those used in RBC production. The white blood cells however do not lose their nuclear or genetic material as do the RBCs. They destroy infections by forming antibodies against them or by physically eating them up. Some cells shoot oxygen radicals at the invading organisms. It is all a bit like "Star Wars".

Likewise, the church sometimes needs to take a fairly aggressive stance against social and moral issues which are undermining our societies, our Christian values and our family life. Some of these issues may include stands against certain social issues such as abortion, apartheid, euthanasia, gambling, pornography, unfair treatment for minority groups such as the aboriginies, immoral standards, unfair business practices, world and local poverty and many others. We need to take an active stance against those issues which, we feel, undermine the values of our society. As one famous man called Edmund Burke once said words to the effect that evil breeds because good men do nothing. So let your politician know when you are unhappy about something instead of sitting around and grumbling about it in a self righteous manner. Too bad if most disagree with you. At least you are standing up for your convictions.

Like the white blood infection fighting cells we can use the word of God like an oxygen radical. Jesus used the word often in his preaching and used it to countermand Satan (Luke 4: 1-13). He certainly was radical in the eyes of the established religion of that time. In fact it was this egoic church that was instrumental in nailing Him to Calvary's Cross.

In addition to the aggressive side of white blood cells they also have another more peaceful function. They release protein factors which help the growth and healing of wounds. They also release factors essential to the normal growth and development of a baby and other white blood cells. We as Christians must also have this function of the white blood cells. The factors that we must put out for the growth and healing of the community is mercy, love, joy, peace, understanding and comfort.

In finishing off this small section it must be stressed that whatever we do in all areas of life needs to be done with guidance from the Holy Spirit which means doing it in a spirit of love. Judging or verbally shooting someone who disagrees with you is not a spirit of love. Having a self righteous, ego-filled attitude is also far from love. We can use the word of God wisely or unwisely. Used wisely it is life giving and unwisely it is not encouraging and imparts guilt and condemnation. The best use of the word of God is us, hopefully living examples of that word. Hopefully with God's grace and help, we will slowly develop into a person like his Son Jesus Christ. That way we will become members of our society who are more able to reflect Jesus Christ to our community.

CHAPTER 4

GASSES OF LIFE AND DEATH

In the animal kingdom, most gasses are lethal and there is only one which is essential to life. This life giving gas is called oxygen and is chemically abbreviated as O-O or O2. The chapter on blood indicated that the main role of this gas is to energise the cell by generating a substance in the cell which is called ATP or adenosine triphosphate. ATP assists hundreds of biochemical reactions to occur in the cell which, with low ATP concentrations, would occur less efficiently resulting eventually in cell death. Oxygen generates this energy producing molecule ATP through a complex biochemical process termed oxidative phosphorylation. In this process, ATP is essentially produced from the metabolism of foods such as sugars, fats and proteins, the body's energy stores. This metabolism results in generation of substances which when oxidised with oxygen (oxidative phosphorylation) produce ATP.

Carbon monoxide or cyanide gases essentially poison the cell by reducing intracellular concentrations of ATP by depleting oxygen availability and by inhibiting oxidative phosphorylation. The body requires vast amounts of ATP daily for its many energy needs not only in muscle related activities but also in various metabolic pathways in the cell such as transporting ions in and out of the cell, forming messenger molecules within the cell, producing genetic material for cell division, energizing hundreds of molecules and metabolic pathways within the cell. Therefore a cell with low levels of ATP or insufficient oxygen is incompatible with life. That is why oxygen deprivation of only 1-2 minutes in humans may result in coma and death.

As indicated, oxygen is involved in generating energy (ATP) through metabolism. The result of metabolism is the production of a gas called carbon dioxide or CO_2. Despite the presence of O_2 in this molecule CO_2 it is incompatible with life in animals. It is however compatible with life in plants. Plants absorb atmospheric CO_2 and convert it into sugar and oxygen using solar energy (a process termed photosynthesis). The plant in turn metabolises this CO_2-derived sugar to derive its own ATP/energy. We and other animals eat these plants and derive energy contained in them. Because excess CO_2 is not compatible with life in animals, the body exhales it from our lungs. And so exhaled breadth is rich in CO_2 and after release into the atmosphere it is absorbed by plants and reconverted into sugar and oxygen as already indicated. So this whole process is a cyclical one.

With lung disease, CO_2 is inefficiently exhaled resulting in increased CO2 within the body. This trapped CO2 is converted within the patient into an acid called carbonic acid which acidifies both the blood and tissues. This increase of acid in the body is serious and may result in death. The human body is intolerant of changes in acidity or, what is technically known as pH or hydrogen ion content. For example the blood normally contains of 35 to 45 nanograms of hydrogen ion per litre. A nanogram is one billionth of a gram (a gram is about 1/30th of an ounce). With a minor change of acidity change to 160 nanograms / litre, the patient will die of excess acidity or acidosis.

Acidosis causes a loss of potassium salt from the cells and body and so the patient becomes hyperkalemic. That is they have high potassium levels in their blood plasma which can cause death. Additionally the normal, efficient cellular enzyme functions in our bodies are affected by acidity. Over acidity ultimately results in impaired enzyme and human function. To conclude, acidosis has numerous, negative side effects on the cells of the body and it is obvious why the human body is so designed so as to rid itself of CO_2.

The term bitter is synonymous with acidity. For example the bitter taste of lemons is due to their high concentrations of organic acids such as tartaric and citric acids. Bitterness in a human being is sometimes said to be synonymous with an acid disposition or hardness of heart. Bitterness in a person is usually due to unforgiveness. For example, people hurt by other people or circumstances can be unforgiving, bitter and become hard hearted.

The Bible has much to say both directly and indirectly about bitterness,hardness of heart and unforgiveness. In the Lord's prayer we are exhorted to forgive those who have trespassed against us as the Lord has forgiven us (Matt 6:8-15). In fact the theme of forgiving and love seems to dominate most of the bible. It seems that one cannot love without forgiving and one cannot forgive without loving. Forgiveness is an important aspect of loving (Luke 7:40-50).

Bitterness in the human emotions is caused by or is the fruit of an unforgiving, revengeful attitude. Like physical bitterness it can inhibit the full development or realization of our inner being or spiritual life. Also it can sap us of our energy because of emotional pain which, if sustained, can cause physical sickness. When CO_2 gas is released into a confined space it causes acidity in humans. Similarly, emotional bitterness can suffocate and influence the lives of those who live near that bitter person. That is people associating with a bitter person can also be influenced to be bitter and critical if they are not emotionally strong or discerning enough to recognize and avoid this negative attitude. Bitterness therefore has a contagious property about it and so one must try and avoid the source of infection or bitter environment unless one is strong or discerning enough to affect a cure. Also bitter people loose their salt or flavour (vitality) or inner beauty just as physical acidity causes loss of potassium salt from the cell.

To summarize, emotional acidity or unforgiveness/bitterness can cause a person to become emotionally sick and lethargic just like insufficient oxygen or excess CO_2 in a person physically depletes the body of ATP, its energy source. In turn bitterness/unforgiveness can be reflected in the physical well being of that person since our emotional and physical health seem to be closely connected. In short, a person can fail, as a result of bitterness, to reach their full potential. That is emotional acidity or an unforgiving attitude can inhibit the development of the positive qualities in the inner being. It is no wonder therefore that the Lord, in His love for us, warns and commands us many times to forgive and love one another (Matt 18:21, 22). Nonetheless, some justify their unforgiveness by using God's word against the offending person such as "As you sow so shall you reap" (2 Cor 9:6) and "If you love someone you discipline them" (Prov 13: 24). However discipline is not condemnation and unloving criticism is usually a mark of unforgiveness. No matter how one tries to justify their stance of unforgiveness, the word of God is very clear on this topic - forgive and love without any caveats. God knows what is good for us.

God warns us to remove the log from our eyes before trying to remove the splinter from our colleague's eye (Luke 6: 41-42). We are also told by loving and not judging anyone we are born of God (1 John 4: 7,8). An act can be judged as unfair or unlawful but only God has the right to judge the attitudes and motives, that is the heart of a person. If we recognize and repent of our unforgiveness, God will forgive and release us from this burden and the process of healing can begin. We can begin to blow off this bitterness or acidity and thereby normalize our relationships with others and with God.

Most of us feel compassion not only for those who have been greatly wronged but also feel for those who have done wrong to another as it can be very difficult to forgive oneself and live with the heavy weight of guilt. If we are willing, the key to being able to forgive ourselves and others is found in scripture. This inspiration came from a sermon heard many years ago.

We know the story of Moses when he led the people of God, the Israelites, from bondage in Egypt to liberty in the land promised by God. One day, people complained to Moses that the waters at a place called Marah were bitter and unsuitable for drinking. God told Moses to throw a piece of wood into the water which then became sweet and suitable to drink (Ex 15: 23-25). Another time, there was no water and God commanded Moses to touch a rock with his staff and water suitable for drinking came out of this rock (Ex 17: 3-7). In the context of these stories, wood or the staff of Moses represents the cross of Christ. If we allow the cross of Christ to touch our hardness, hurts and bitterness, Jesus is able to make something useful and sweet out of them just like plant life converts our physical bitterness (CO_2) into sugar and oxygen. The only priviso is that if we are willing to let go of our hurts and give them to Jesus, God will make something good (sweet) out of something bad (acid). We are not asked to forget as that would be very difficult if not impossible. Time however will dim the memory.

Jesus is a wonderful example of forgiveness not only throughout his life on earth but particularly on the cross of Calvary. He had been physically abused and humiliated by the Roman soldiers. This abuse included a crown of thorns brutally pushed into His head, being whipped 39 times till the skin was ripped from His back, had His beard ripped off, being verbally abused, spat upon and ridicucled by the priests and people about Him. The abuse and humiliation came to a peak at the crucifixtion (Isa 50: 4-6; Isa 53). In addition, and even worse, He took all our sins and diseases on His body (Col 2:13-15; 1 Peter 2:24-25; Rev 1: 4-9; Heb 2:17). He could have side stepped this excruciating pain and humiliation of both body and spirit. His heavenly Father would have rescued Him and destroyed all those about Him if Jesus had called on Him. Christ went through all of this physical and spiritual pain to show God's immense love for us and to deliver us from our sins (John 3:16). His desire for us was to have us reconciled to Him (God) in peace and blessings and love for all eternity (1 Peter 3:9; Heb 6:7,14 ; 1 John 4: 10 - 20).

While on earth Jesus healed the sick, raised the dead, fed those who were physically and spirititually hungry and most importantly gave those about Him hope, joy, love and peace. Jesus was without sin and completely innocent so His death was certainly unjustified and in fact the most horrendous injustice ever perpertrated (1 Peter 1:21-23;

Heb 4:15; Rom 5: 12-21). Despite all of this, as He hung from that blood stained cross, His body and spirit wracked with indescribable physical and spiritual pain, He cried "Father forgive them, they know not what they do" (Luke 23: 34). That was the infinite example of forgiveness and agape love. One can argue that Jesus was God and so it was easy for Him to forgive. Yes He is God, but He laid aside His Godhead when he came to earth and became fully man (Acts 2: 22-40; Col 1 : 16-22). He hurt,He cried, He felt pain, He grieved, He felt joy, He was an emotional human being like us (Matt 26:28; Luke 19: 41; John 11: 35; 15:11). Even before His torture and crucifixation, His emotional agony was such as He faced the cross that He sweated drops of blood (Luke 22: 44). How many of us have come to that point of suffering and stress in our lives?

Forgiveness is not easy. After becoming a Christian in July 1977, there were about 9 people who I considered my enemies and asked them for their forgiveness. To put it mildly, dialling their phone numbers was very hard to do. But afterwards there was a tremendous relief and healing taking place within me. The peace and love of God absolutely overwhelmed me so much to the point of crying. As a Christian unjust treatment many times have come my way. After much soul searching and frustration, one eventually learns to identify the hurt, repent and then leave any negative feelings and sinful thoughts at the cross of Christ. What has been a considerable help was to pray for blessings and the salvation of those who wronged me. Pray has also included a changed Christ-like attitude on my behalf toward them. When doing so, a loving feeling toward that person may evolve after a while. It is a daily grind sometimes to be a good Christian but with the Holy Spirit's help God can effect positive changes to our lives. Almost daily, the egoic part of me judges people (and many other misdemeanors) and one has to continually remind oneself that God is the judge. God certainly is longsuffering with me.

When a patient can't breathe properly (emphysema or asthma) or has taken an overdose of a poisonous gas carbon monoxide (suicide attempt or fire victim) the treatment involves the introduction of pure oxygen to that patient to blow off the CO_2 and carbon monoxide (CO) stored in the body's tissues. In fact, with CO poisoning, the patient must be treated with oxygen delivered at high pressure. To do this they use a chamber called the hyperbaric or high pressure oxygen chamber. This hyperbaric treatment with oxygen is needed otherwise CO is not completely removed from the inner body stores and is subsequently released slowly from internal organs and tissues causing the patient to relapse later. Therefore, the high pressure oxygen removes residual CO thereby preventing any further relapse.

In both a spiritual and psychological context, we can be polluted by the CO-like poisons of society such as pornography, violence, drugs and childhood abuses. All these sinful events, can have negative effects on our attitudes and can leave us in fear, insecurity and torment as well as give us a distorted view of life. If they occur early in life, when we lack the maturity to handle them, they can cause serious psychological damage. God in His wonderful provision has made a way. He said that He came that we may have life and have it more abundantly (John 10: 10). He also said that His words are spirit and life (John 6:63). God's word to the spiritual body is what oxygen is to the physical body. If we allow His word to permeate (not glance off) our spirit, it will heal us by blowing out all the life-accumulated junk in us. We need to take in God's word daily in faith thereby allowing it to penetrate our innermost being. Just like oxygen in order to energize the cell (ie generate ATP) must get into the innermost organelles of the cell (mitochondria), so must the word of God be welcomed and embraced by us to penetrate our innermost being in order to blow out the polluting influences in our spiritual bodies and, thereby, effectively work in our lives.

How do you take God's word in faith? By knowing that Jesus Christ loves you and wants your happiness more than you do. That Jesus knows what will make you happy even though you do not understand what or why He is doing or allowing certain things to happen in your life for a good reason. That is for your spiritual sanctfication and growth. By knowing that Holy Scripture is not a series of dos and donts but a message of love from God where He is saying follow my words and you will be happy. By knowing that God laws are there to reflect our sinful nature and thereby appreciate and be grateful for forgiveness and salvation through faith in Jesus Christ. To understand the depth of love God has for us.

Without being energized the person cannot be healed. As the physical body requires ATP energy to do its many functions so the human soul needs to be energized by God's Word in order to be healed. In order for the healing process to occur in our emotions we need an energized positive spirit or attitude which only the word of God can give. If we do not internalise God's word, that is we read His book the Bible like a novel or an interesting story then it will not do its work fully though it may still have a positive influence in our lives. God speaks through his word to us so that we will be changed for the better.

There can be blocks in our life to receiving God's Word fully. We may have had some Satanic involvement or lived a life full of sin. Repentance from these will remove the blocks to God's Word. Sometimes the block can be your low self esteem, a feeling that we have failed, life has passed us by, we deserve nothing, God doesn't or couldn't really love me. That latter comment is a lie from Hell because God loved us so much that He died a horrendous and humilating death for us. To love yourself is in fact is one of the foremost commandments of God along with loving God and your neighbour (Matt 22:36-40). You are lovable because you are made in the image of God and you are unique and very precious because God will never make another like you

These negative feelings of low self esteem Satan would have us believe is a mark of humility. True humility is when you acknowledge God as the source of all your positive attributes and that you are a unique, one-off person created by God.

Sinfulness, egoism (self hate and low self esteem or false self exultation) is like the thick mucous lining the lungs in an asthmatic. It prevents the oxygen or the word of God from energizing you. Give all the glory to Christ for all the unique and wonderful qualities that

He has built into you. It may help to make a list of your qualities and thank God for them. Like the apostle Paul we very likely may also have thorns in our flesh (weaknesses). Like Paul know that God's grace is sufficient for us (2 Cor 12, 7-9) and also ask God for help with our negatives (and we all have them unfortunately) without magnifying them any more. Knowing that God has created us a unique human being in His image and that we are His children is more than anyone could hope for. Knowing this will help change and transform your view of life and yourself since being called God's child is the highest accolade on this planet. If you saw your kids running themselves down all the time it wouldn't make you happy. More so with God.

Having a deep walk with Holy Spirit in our lives will help the word to penetrate as deep as the bone marrow of our spiritual lives (Heb 4: 12). Faith is the key ingredient in all of this healing process. If you have faith as a mustard seed, faith that Christ wants the best for you life, then the word will move the mountains of pollution out of your life and make you whole (Matt 17:20). The Holy Spirit indwelling within us allows this faith to grow as He teaches us about Jesus (Heb 12:2; Acts 15:8,9; Jude 20). After all He inspired the bible (2 Tim 3: 16) through the writings of various authors so He certainly knows the correct interpretation and He will make known God's word to us in a deep and meaningful way which is life transforming, that is depolluting. In a polluted world like ours isn't it wonderful that we have the greatest purifying and depolluting agent, the mighty word of God taught to us by the wonderful Holy Spirit, the third person of the Blessed Trinity? It cannot get better than that.

It is a sad observation that many who have lacked love and acceptance early in their lives can subsequently become bitter and hurt, unfortunately sometimes attempting to numb this pain with drugs. These drugs are usually addictive and, in general, are basic substances or bases. (Substances chemically opposite to acids are called bases). These bases can neutralize or reduce acidity. Drugs such as heroin, morphine, cocaine, LSD, nicotine and amphetamines are all bases. The trouble with these drugs is that they are addictive and have negative effects on your personality. Sure, they temporarily kill the emotional pain but at a somewhat horrendous cost to your life. That is the costs of taking these drugs far outweighs the questionable benefits received by taking them. An advertisement seen at a bus stop a few years ago stuck with me. The ad showed a young man taking drugs with a caption below which read "Tim's need for heroin is only exceed by his need for love". That caption said it all. Lack of love/acceptance can lead to bitterness and emotional pain which is partially neutralised by the addictive bases. Knowing the extent of the love and acceptance Our Lord Jesus Christ has for us is an important milestone in our healing. So great is His love for us that He died for us a terrible and ghastly death on a wooden cross outside of Jerusalem 2,000 years ago. Not only that but He also took all our bitterness, emotional and physical pain, guilt and sin to that cross and crucified it as well on His body (1 Peter 2:21-24; Isa 53: 5-12).

When we acknowledge our sinfulness and accept Christ as our Lord and Saviour, when we put our lives into His hands, it is important to accept and tell Our loving Father about our fears and pain (He wants us to talk with Him about it even though He knows everything) and to hand Him all our hurts. As we become aware of His love for us, as we get to know Him more our pain will diminish. As the scripture says "for by His wounds you were healed" (1 Peter 2:24). In this healing process it is probably important to relate our pain to another human as well as to God. Hence, we may need psychological counselling in this healing process as well. The healing process is a gradual process and we have the assurance that Jesus touches not only our emotional scars immediately but also this healing touch continues throughout our lives as we continue to trust in Him and His provisions for our lives (Mark 11:24,25). Knowing the extent of His love for us as expressed in Holy Scripture and having a personal relationship with Christ through frank and open discussions in prayer will increase our faith and our healing. Christ's plan for your life is that you may have life and have it more abundantly (John 10: 10). So trust in Him. There are millions of dedicated Christians can vouch for His wonderful provisions in their lives. The greatest provision is having God in the centre of our lives. It makes all the difference.

The peace Christ gives is deep and lasting. It must be experienced personally. As He said "My peace I give to you; not as the world gives, do I give to you" (John 14: 27). The peace of the world is transient and usually short-lived. Christ's peace starts deep within us and it makes us feel complete or whole. It gives a deep inner strength no matter what the circumstance or whereever you have come from. Christ healing is real through the love He pours into us.

There are situations pertaining to forgiveness which probably need some elaboration or explanation. Where a partner is chronically abusive then for your own physical and emotional well being you should leave that person. By chronically abusive I mean that she or he continually beats or abuses you either physically or emotionally and makes your life a living hell to the point that your self image is so negative and you cannot cope anymore. You have to love yourself and any children you may have to get out of that poisonous situation. There is little hope for reconciliation if that partner is unwilling to admit their faults and accept change for their life by refusing to come for counselling. For it is only at the cross that Christ can deal with our attitudes and shortcomings if we will allow Him. Also we have to be truthful about ourselves and also recognize that we need to change. It is sometimes very easy to see the splinter in our brother's eye but do nothing about the log in ours. Even though you may leave your spouse it is very important that you forgive him/her and yourself as well. The bitterness and hurt of the marriage must be left at the foot of the cross.

Every domestic situation must be carefully looked at by competent counsellors and assessed accurately in the light of God's word. Whatever the circumstance, it is essential to love and forgive the erring partner in your heart. By doing so it will allow you to rebuild your own life. If possible explain to them that you have to live separately from him/her for your own sanity. You should of course pray for that partner and should they come to a full and genuine repentance then you should accept them back. By their fruits over a period of time you will know that there has been a genuine repentance (Matt 7: 15-20).

In all written so far the two main players in this drama is you and God. Scripture encourages to have a close walk with Christ and His word in order that you may be made whole. At times, a Christian counsellor may be needed in this healing process, usually someone who you can relate to and feel comfortable with to discuss your problems. Someone to pray for you and be a support. Such counsellors and friends have been a blessing to me. On the other hand some have lacked wisdom and have almost shaken me from my Christian walk. Time will tell whether your counsellor is suitable for you. As God says by their fruits you shall know them (Matt 7: 15-20). The fruits may take a while to become evident, so be patient and try not to be judgemental. Your counsellor is as human as you and needs as much pray. So pray that they may be led by God. A little revelation from God can work wonders and is worth a mountain of human wisdom.

I would like now to digress by symbolizing some of the gasses so far discussed. This symbolism, which came to me one morning while walking, is important in that it relates to this discussion on gasses. As indicated, oxygen O2 or O-O is like the word of God by being life giving. Oxygen, denoted by a circle O, is without beginning or end like God. A ring (circle) is used to indicate our love for someone. The poisonous gases carbon monoxide or CO and carbon dioxide or CO2 may be likened to the contaminated word hence the symbol C attached to oxygen. The contaminated word can be scripture taken out of context so that it no longer gives life. For example some Christians believe that speaking in tongues is a sign of salvation and quote a scripture from Mark to support their belief (Mark 16: 17). Faith scriptures can be taken out of context. For example some parents wont take their very sick child to the doctor believing that God alone will heal and they use scripture to justify their stance. Some Christians use scripture to prohibit life saving blood transfusion since they believe that any blood transfusion will somehow damn your soul and later on prohibit entry into Heaven. The other way of contaminating scripture is to quote it but do not live by it. It is harder to walk the talk than talk the walk. For example one may say that they have forgiven their wife's infidelity but then keep reminding her daily or weekly. Jesus was angry with Pharisees because they quoted scripture self righteously but never abided by the essence of the law which is love (Matt 6: 1 - 16; 15: 7; 23: 13-36; Luke 11: 38-54). It is symbolic that the carbon atom attached to the oxygen atom is black and oxidizing agents containing oxygen tend to bleach or whiten. Hence CO and CO2, though poisonous, are colourless indicating that the blackness is overcome by the light.

Water has interesting physical and spiritual aspects. It is also talked about in God's word as also being synonymous with life and in the physical we can relate to that (John 4: 7-15; Rev 21:6; 22: 1,17). Water has the formula H2O or H-O-H. Here God, represented again by the circle, is attached to humanity represented by the symbol H. It is water which exclusively quenches our thirst. Likewise humanity joined to God is life giving. The elements of hydrogen and oxygen when brought together as gasses do not bond spontaneously. If you are foolhardy and apply a spark to this mixture of gasses they will bond together instanteously in an explosive manner and form water. It is the energy of this bonding through hydrogen peroxide or H-O-O-H that energises spaceships. God is waiting to bond to us. It just takes a spark from us (a "yes") to do it. Once this bond is formed between God and us like water it is very difficult to disrupt. What will disrupt this bond is chronic disrespect and disobedience to God's laws and one can do this only if they do not have a deep relationship with God. However God will do all He can to stop this happening without encroaching on our free will.

Oxygen is called electronegative. That means it attracts negatively charged particles called electrons from atoms like hydrogen (H2). When God (O2) bonds with humanity (H2) to give water (life) He removes an electron from hydrogen (us). In other words God removes our negativity and makes us positive. Also water is balanced in that it is neither acidic or basic. It is neutral and therefore non- destructive.

In life there are similar chemicals to water called hydrogen sulphide (H2S) or hydrogen selenide (H2Se). These substances are poisonous gasses and have the vilest of stenches (H2S is described as rotten egg gas). In these structures the element S could be symbolic of satan. There is no substitute for water in cleansing and healing, it is everywhere on earth. Without water there is no life. Just so humanity without this bonding to God is also lifeless.

To conclude living the word of God frees us from contaminations in our spirit just as taking in oxygen overcomes the harmful effects of acidity and poisonous gasses. The Holy Spirit helps internalize and bond the word of God deep in our spirits to energize and set us free spiritually. Secondly at the cross of Christ we repent and lay down our hurts regardless of who is right or wrong. At repentance we need to know that God forgives us and will help give us a forgiving heart toward that person involved. Pray also God's richest blessings on your enemies and God will release that bitterness from you and convert it to a sweet fruit in your own life that will be used to feed not only you but also to counsel and energize others in similar circumstances.

We decide whether we want to forgive and love someone. It is not for us to avenge; that is God's business (Deut 32: 35; Psalm 94:1; Heb 10: 30). Once we forgive and love others and ourselves then the peace and love of Almighty God will flood our beings and we shall know true peace. A forgiving and loving heart will deepen our relationship with God.

CHAPTER 5

NUTRITION

We have discussed how humans obtain energy to function through oxygen and food intake. The significance of oxygen has been discussed (gasses) and in this section food intake and/or nutrition will be considered. Humans need a balanced food intake for growth and survival. The major constituents in food comprise proteins, vitamins, carbohydrates and fats all of which are needed for energy and further protein synthesis.

Vitamins are required for a variety of biochemical processes to occur. For example vitamins B1 and B6 are required for biochemical reactions within the cell involving sugar metabolism in order to generate energy and make amino acids for protein synthesis. Vitamin C, also called ascorbic acid, together other reducing agents protects the environment in the cell from damage due to oxidizing species such as oxygen and hydroxy radicals. Vitamin C is also involved in the synthesis of a unique amino acid called hydroxy proline. This amino acid is used to make the protein/collagen matrix between cells. Vitamin C deficiency leads to a lack of proper extracellular matrix, a medical condition commonly called scurvy. Vitamin A is involved not only in the visual process but also used in repairing epithelial cell damage and ensuring normal cell development. Vitamin A deficiency leads to impaired vision at night (night blindness). Vitamin D helps in the absorption of calcium from the gut for bone synthesis. Vitamin D deficiency results in Ricketts a condition in which the bones become brittle and break easily. Vitamin K is used to activate proteins involved in the blood coagulation. Vitamin K deficiency can result in excessive blood loss and death. Vitamins B12 and folate are used for the synthesis of red and white blood cells and other rapidly dividing cells in the body (mouth and gut). A deficiency of these vitamins can result in anaemia and other serious medical complications.

For normal body function, a balance of all these food nutrients is needed. Despite what some may say about the negative aspects of any food sub-group, such as sugar and cholesterol being bad for you, we do need some of these "bad" constituents in order to maintain normal body health. It is only when our intake of these foods exceeds our requirements can they harm us. Conversely a deficiency of most food groups will lead eventually to clinical problems. This deficiency may not necessarily be caused by poor dietary intake but may be due to an abnormal metabolism of these constituents. I shall now attempt to show how nutrient deficiences or poor metabolism may result in serious health problems. I shall not attempt to discuss all the known diet related deficiencies as there are many hundreds of them.

Most people are aware that the hormone insulin is produced by the pancreas and enables the energy-producing sugar glucose to enter certain cells of the body. Lack of this hormone results in the person being unable to absorb glucose. This condition is called Diabetes Mellitus. One variant of this disease is called "Mature Onset Diabetes" as it generally occurs in adults. In this, the patient produces insulin but their cells are resistant to the action of insulin in being able to facilitate glucose entry into the cell. Another variant of this is called "Juvenile Onset Diabetes" as it usually occurs in the young. In this, patients have lost the ability to produce the hormone insulin due to a damaged pancreas. Thus a major effect of Diabetes is the accumulation of glucose outside of the cell. This excess of extracellular glucose then reacts with proteins of the body to form glucose-protein adducts or as is sometimes described, glycated proteins. Glycation of proteins by glucose can contribute to a variety of detrimental clinical conditions such as heart and kidney diseases and blindness. Because the patients cannot absorb glucose into their cells its concentration outside the cells (extracellular) rises in blood. The body tries to get rid of the excess glucose by excreting it into urine. Hence people with Diabetes urinate more than a normal healthy population and thereby lose body water. It is for this reason that diabetics are frequently thirsty when their blood glucose rises. It is the response of their bodies to get rid of the excess glucose building up in their blood.

Poor metabolism of protein products can also result in a variety of serious medical problems. Proteins are composed of smaller molecules called amino acids which if not properly metabolised can result in many medical problems. For example if the amino acid cysteine is not absorbed normally by the kidneys from urine then it may precipitate in urine to give cystine stones with kidney damage resulting. Malabsorption of fats from the gut can also result in serious medical consequences. For example in normal diets, calcium binds a small molecule called oxalate in the gut thereby inhibiting its efficient absorption from the gut and subsequent excretion into urine. When fat is malabsorbed or poorly absorbed from the gut it binds calcium at this site. As a consequence, less oxalate is bound to calcium thereby allowing more oxalate to be absorbed from the gut and be subsequently excreted into urine. Once in urine, where excess calcium is normally present, oxalate will precipitate as its insoluble calcium oxalate salt resulting in the formation of kidney stones. Malabsorption of fats also results in other deficiencies of the fat soluble vitamins A,D,E and K. That is these vitamins need normal fat absorption in order to be absorbed.

A protein called intrinsic factor is made by stomach cells and is used to bind and help absorb vitamin B12 from the gut. A key function of vitamin B12 is in the production of red blood cells. Thus patients who lack intrinsic factor and consequently normal B12 absorption eventually become B12 deficient and anaemic, a condition called Pernicious Anaemia. That is, their blood haemoglobin levels become low and they become very tired. The treatment is to give patients an intramuscular injection of vitamin B12 thereby repleating their low B12 stores in the body and bypassing the defunct intrinsic factor pathway.

Previous research done with colleagues showed that patients unable to absorb ascorbate efficiently tend to form renal stones. We showed that the unabsorbed ascorbate is converted to oxalate in the gut and this oxalate eventually finds its way into the urine where it precipitates to form oxalate kidney stones.

To conclude, there are many clinical conditions characterised by either poor metabolism or absorption of certain foodstuffs. This in turn results in a variety of serious medical complications which can cause considerable pain and discomfort to the patient and sometimes death.

In the Bible, Jesus refers to two foods from heaven. One, called manna, was used to feed the Jews in the desert when they left Egypt with Moses (Ex 16:35; John 6:31, 49). The other is a food which is spiritually good for us. Jesus says that He is that spiritual food and goes on to state that anyone eating His body and blood would not die but have eternal life (John 6: 47-58). At this stage many of His followers left Him probably because they thought He was advocating cannabalism. What Jesus was implying was that He is the Word of God sent from heaven and anyone taking this Word into their inner most being or the depths of their spirit would be spiritually energized even for eternity.

Jesus stated that His words are spirit and life (John 6: 63). The Bible also says that the Word of God will get down into the inner most parts of us if we will allow it (Heb 4:12). To emphasize this, holy scripture says that it will even pierce the division of soul and spirit. This Word has a wonderful effect on us. Jesus says out of our inner most being shall flow rivers of living water (John 4:10; 7: 38). Water is a necessity of life. The living water that Jesus was talking about was the Holy Spirit (John 7:39). With the Holy Spirit or living water in our lives, we can help heal and cleanse those around us. The word of God or Holy Scripture is, without doubt, the most wonderful and only real food for our spirits. It takes the Holy Spirit to make God's Word real to us. It took me a long period (40 years plus) of my life to come to that realization. Let me just change tack for a moment to explain my initial views about the word of God. This diversion though a little egoic is important to the discussion on nutrition so please bear with me.

The Word of God was always in our home. It was in the form of a huge, impressive, gold Catholic Bible. We would dust this Bible and now and then, when there was a blue moon about, we would dare to open its hallowed pages. In those days, 5 minutes reading was enough to send us to sleep. The book was unreal, a fairy story. How could the whole population come from one man and woman - ridiculous (see Chapter 2). It seemed inconceivable that the whole world could flood and that a man could live in the belly of a whale for three days. How could Noah get all those animals into one boat without them all eating up each other? What about evolution did it not discredit the whole Bible story of creation? In my so called wisdom, the conclusion was formed that the Bible had some interesting stories but that it did not bear any relevance to this modern day and age. However the words of Jesus had a nice ring to them. He seemed a good bloke, seemed to do a lot of miracles and good things which helped those about Him. But that was 2,000 years ago and not very relevant for today.

At the same time one wasn't sure what was relevant for today. Perhaps science and technology are. Yes Jesus was a good bloke but He really was God and not really one of us struggling mortals. Sure the Jews were a bit stupid putting Him on a cross. Perhaps they were jealous of Him or perhaps they were just plain thick. Anyway who cares as there are so many other interesting things to do in life. Like go to parties and dances and get drunk. Or go and kick a football or play tennis or golf. There was no harm in these activities except perhaps getting drunk. Anyway, these superficial thoughts summarized my view of the Bible and the stories contained therein. The Bible to my way of thinking was not relevant to today's world.

However, my life seemed to be leading nowhere. There was a emptiness there which was filled up with things which really did not satisfy or give a lasting peace. Things like materialism, alcohol and infidelity, things which all fed the flesh and not the spirit. Yes, Ainsley was an intellectually orientated person who thought he figured out what was the logical way to go or the thing to do. On the surface, I looked happy and successful with a lovely wife, 3 gorgeous daughters, a good job, a nice house and car. This facade of my life however lead to a great deal of frustration and pain not only to myself but to those close to me. Within, I was a tormented person but outwardly was wearing a mask of happiness and success.

A major change occurred in my life when I gave my life to Christ and accepted Him into my heart to be my Lord and Saviour. Sure it is one thing to call Christ "Lord" in church once a week but another thing to really mean it in the depths of your being. To actually put the Lord on the throne of your life and make Him central to everything was something else. When this decision was made there was immediately a deep peace which came upon me. A deep peace previously never known. Later my Christian walk received another boost when I received through prayer a fresh infilling of the Holy Spirit as is described in scripture (Acts 1: 5,8, 2: 4,38, 4: 8,31; Luke 11: 13, 3:16). With these two experiences came a close presence of the Lord in my life. One knew without a shadow of doubt that Jesus is the way the truth and the life and that the other options that life held were not worth any consideration.

The Word of God became real. All those misconceptions about the Word disappeared. These were exciting times, fed and brought to life by His word. My spirit was enlivened and energized. This gift was from God. He had promised it to those who would ask in His name. There was very little effort on my part, just a decision to invite Him into my life in a deeper way with the prompting of a pastor. His gift or grace did the rest. I knew at that moment that I was now His child, that His mark was on me, that salvation was eternally mine (Eph 1:13; 4:30; 2 Cor 1:22; 1 Cor 9:2; 2 Tim 2:19). Cleanliness and purity became part of my being not because of myself but because of Him. I was getting full of the Word of God and hungry to learn more.

What has this all got to do with nutrition? In my pre- or early christian life there was a need to work to gain merit or favour with God. Over the years this wore me out spiritually. It became a chore and a frustration because one could never, by nature, meet the requirements of the law and God, to my way of thinking, was a hard task master. I was like the apostle Paul trying to do good but being frustrated by falling down all the time (Rom 7). Like vitamin C and fat malabsorption, if we do not take the Word or Manna of God fully into our beings then we can develop stones in our spiritual beings. These stones can cause a great deal of pain just like renal stones cause physical pain. Also these stones impede the flow of living water from Christ and as a consequence cannot clear out the junk in us. Similarly when we do not absorb the word, like glucose in diabetes, then we lose water and become dry and thirsty spiritually.

When you allow the goodness of God to permeate your inner most being you really feel nourished. All you have to do is to receive God's blessing. If you do not allow the fullness of God to permeate you then you are not absorbing His spiritual nutrition fully. It is there but you lack the receptors to take it into your being. Or rather you are unaware that these receptors are there. You just have to be willing to receive from God. He does the rest. It is a gift. It is His grace earned for you at Calvary 2,000 years ago but still ever present today. As Christ promised, out of you shall flow rivers of living water. These waters clean out the rubbish in your life, they heal and nourish you. If these waters are not flowing then you develop spiritual renal stones. The junk in your spiritual life cannot be cleared. You feel contaminated. There is a great deal of spiritual pain and morbity which is expressed in your emotions. Yes we need to absorb fully the Word of God and the person of His Son Jesus Christ to be fully released and nourished in the inner most part of us. It is the one instance where gluttony is allowed. We really cannot have enough of the Christlife expressed in His Word. The Word truly is spirit and life to us.

Absorbing the Word of God is also like absorbing iron from our food. Remember in the chapter on blood how iron is an important part of haemoglobin which is in the red blood cell and that the haemoglobin is a type of the Holy Ghost which carries the word or oxygen equivalent to tissues deprived of it. There are many food constituents which inhibit the absorption of the much needed iron from the gut. One food group which stands out are the acids present in food such as phytate, tannate and oxalate. Without proper absorption of iron, we cannot make red blood cells and we become anaemic and as a result feel weak and lack energy. The best absorbed form of iron in foodstuffs is haemoglobin present in meat and fish. Iron represents the Word of God and haemoglobin the Holy Ghost. Therefore to absorb the Word of God into our spirits we need the Holy Spirit attached to the Word. All other things (intellect, worldly pollutions, bitterness, pride) in this world tend to inhibit this process. Also acids in food inhibit iron absorption. In our spiritual life unforgiveness and bitterness are like acids (see chapter on gasses) and these negative emotions unless resolved will inhibit the full absorption of the Word of God. Before I came to Christ, there were "my enemies". They had done me wrong in my eyes and in no way was any forgiveness due to them in my equation. After coming to Christ, the Holy Spirit prompted me to ring up each one and asked them to forgive me of my negative attitude toward them. Let me add that this wasn't an easy process. However having done this the peace of God flooded me and there was a huge spiritual release within me. Tears of joy and peace flowed thereby releasing me.

As indicated, there are a number of blocks to receiving this nourishment from God. Maybe our intellect is so highly tuned that we have rationalized God almost out of existence. God is not revealed to the intellect. He communicates with the inner being or spirit. Our intellect interprets the revelation of God to the inner being and must be subservient to it. There is nothing wrong with study and developping the intellect. It is a good worthwhile pursuit and most importantly it is a gift from God which we are encouraged to use by God (Prov 1:2-7, 4:5, 9:9, 10:14, 17:27). But it must be balanced and not be allowed to rule the whole person. As an example there is a colleague of mine who is a brilliant scientist. When sharing with great excitement my recent Christian conversion to him, he impressed me by quoting great slabs of scripture to me and related how he had spent 12 years of his life in a christian school. Initial rejoicing was followed by confusion when he told me he was an atheist. For a long time this news was hard to figure out, until the realization came that the Word of God was in his head but not his spirit or heart.

The theory of evolution though sounding very plausible and palatable is popular with most academics and intellectuals. I have found it a major trap for people not coming to Christ. It certainly was for me and many of my scientific colleagues. However as you go into the truth of it you find it is the greatest lie perpetrated by Satan as it blocks many from coming to Christ. My warning is if the word of God describes something like creation for example then don't throw it out because many intellectuals have done so or it is popular to do so. In time you will come to know that God's word is the truth and anything which contradicts it is a lie. It has taken me many years to find this out. Just remember that "the foolishness of God is wiser than men; and the weakness of God is stronger than men" (1 Cor 1:25) and that in God is hidden all treasures of wisdom and knowledge (Col2;3).

Another intellectual trap is to point the finger at ministers or Christians who have fallen and then justify why one wouldn't want to be a hypocrite like that. In other words we throw out the baby with the bath water. Our walk with the Lord should be steadfast regardless of who falls. God is not going to judge us on whether some minister fell from grace. He is going to judge us on what we have done with our lives. If someone falls we should pray and support them. They are human and must be hurting. God said that we are not to judge others as that is his realm (Deut 32:35; Psalm 94:1,2; Heb 10: 30).

The other block is in the area of sensibility. Perhaps we have been sexually abused as a child and have a poor image of a male or father. As a child Catholic Nuns and Brothers were my teachers. In those days (1940s and 50s) those people were very cruel and beat us incessantly for only minor misdemeanors. For example, one brother used to make me stand on my desk and shout to the whole class that I was a donkey while he whacked me repeatedly on the legs with a cane. Later the scripture showed me that the donkey was a Christ bearer on Psalm Sunday. So being a donkey was not so bad. The other teachers humilated me before the class by nicknaming me rajah and asking if an elephant brought me to school or where were my bows and arrows as our family had recently emigrated from India. It was a bit much for a 10 year old to cop all this nonsense. For these sorts of reasons, we may be distrustfull of God because of His male figure portrayed in scripture. A person such as this can come to healing by having a full understanding of the unconditional love of God and by acceptance of Him. Most importantly they need to forgive those who have hurt him/her in the past and ask God to bless them. Healing in this area came to me through counselling, repentance, prayer and laying on of hands. Perhaps we have grown up with only a little love in our lives. We have never been mothered and cuddled. All these experiences can make us feel unworthy and thereby cause us to shut ourselves from the love of God, the love of others and the love of ourselves. People such as these with hurt sensibilities can sometimes try and kill the hurt with suicide, alcohol or drugs. A close friend of mine tried all of these but thank God he survived and is now going on with Christ as a whole person

Another block to receiving the spiritual nutrition of God fully could be because of sickness to our body. Perhaps we have had years of asthma and our lives have been debilitated by it. Generally people blame God and harden their hearts toward Him. Maybe someone has lost a loved one through an accident, divorce or sickness and is bitter for this reason. Perhaps someone can see around us the misery and suffering of humanity and wonder about the so called love of God. These are all very natural feelings and it is very hard to explain suffering in one paragraph. Many excellent books have been written on this subject by Christian counsellors. Suffering, though a part of our fallen state, does however play a role in making us more compassionate. We must accept it when it comes as it does ultimately help us in our growth and learning about life. As the bible says everthing works for good for those following the Lord (Rom 8:28). Hiding will not make it go away. We need to face it and be wholly aware of it. By such actions it will slowly disappear. All I can say is that Christ suffered as a human being for us and out of love for us. He can therefore empathise with

63

us in our suffering. Perhaps, more importantly, I can empathise with Christ and others through my suffering. Also the whole gospel story shouts life and not death. Christ is a life-giving person. He uplifted all who came to Him. His words are spirit and they are life (John 6; 63). Finally God's ways are not our ways. It gets very frustrating and counterproductive trying to figure out why things happen sometimes. Just let God be God of your life after all he is love (1 John 4:8). Accepting the mysteries or unexplainable is part of the faith walk with Christ. God made this very clear to Job (Job 40-42). If we are bitter against God we have to repent and ask His forgiveness. Once again we have to forgive ourselves.

Is my life one series of blisses one after another after becoming a Christian in the true sense of the word? No way. My marriage of nearly 28 years ended when my wife died of cancer at a young age of 48 years. She died whilst I was trying to start writing this book. My heart was shattered by it for many years. I loved her dearly. She was instrumental in my becoming a Christian and a continual inspiration of faith in God to me. I praise God for the gift of her life to our family. Through the emotional pain of this loss and intense grief, a lot of emotions within me surfaced. The Lord has had to deal with a lot of childhood hurts in my sensibility and with a lot of programmed wrong thinking in my intellect. Repentance and forgiveness have become a daily ritual with me. Praise God that we are growing more and more into Him through all of this pain from the past.

As the Lord has said, once He has started a work in you He will complete it (Phil 1:6). Yes nearly all of us have had a lot of emotional pain to cope with but we are bouyed by the knowledge that the God of this universe is love and is with us always. He lives in us and He loves us more than we can ever begin to realize. He is continually healing us day by day. That is His plan and that is His nature. His word continues to abide and to help us grow in our inner being. Yes He continues to feed and nourish day by day and so we praise Him continually for His mighty grace and mercy and peace.

CHAPTER 6

THE SIGNIFICANCE OF SALT

There are many different salts present in the human body. These salts are found all over the body in the blood, organs, tissues and limbs. The most prominent of all these salts outside the cell is a substance called sodium chloride. Within the cell, another salt called potassium chloride has the highest concentration. In addition to potassium and sodium chloride there are other salts such as ammoniun, magnesium and calcium salts. The salt I shall refer to the most in this chapter is sodium chloride which has the highest concentration by far of any other salt in blood plasma. This is the salt we have on our dining tables at home, use as a flavouring agent and refer to it as common salt.

Salt can be crystalized from water to give a beautiful cube-shaped crystal. Salt crystals also transmit light even low energy or infra red light. It also reflects light from its crystal faces and this is what gives it its diamond like beauty. Salt crystals are used in the laboratory because they have the unique property of letting through light of a wide energy spectrum. By comparison glass will only allow a narrow window of visible light energy to pass through.

The other interesting aspect of salt is that it has antiseptic properties when dissolved in water. Some of us for example have gargled with salt when we have had a sore throat or used it to get rid of mouth ulcers. Also the curative properties of the sea is attributed to its salt content. In addition to its antiseptic properties salt can be used as a cleaning agent. Perhaps its greatest use is in the kitchen where it is used as a flavouring agent. Salt is also used for preserving certain foodstuffs or pickling.

In human blood and other tissues salt plays a very important physiological role. It is present in blood plasma at a concentration of about 8.4 grams/litre. This represents nearly one level teaspoonsful of salt for every litre of blood plasma. Its function in blood and cells in general is to maintain the osmolality. What this means is that if its concentration gets too low or high then the blood cells of the body will burst open. Before this happens, the patient can become very sick and die even if there is only a minor change of about 10 % in blood salt concentration.

Salts are also involved in transmitting signals from the brain through the nerve cells to the receptor tissues such as muscle. So the salt concentration is very vital to the normal functionning of the human body and the human body will not tolerate even small fluctuations in its salt concentrations as it is the key ingredient in maintaining the osmolality of the body fluids. For example, when you get thirsty it is because the salt concentration in your blood has risen. The thirst centres in the brain recognize this change in the blood salt concentration and urges you you to drink water. Conversely when you have drunk too much water and the salt concentration is too low, your kidneys will ensure that all that excess water will be got rid of.

Salt in all its functions is associated with water. You taste its flavour because it dissolves in the water on your tongue. If salt was as soluble as sand it would not have any flavour as indeed pure sand does not have. In its physiological role in the body, salt is dissolved in the water compartment of blood and cells. Wherever salt goes so does water and vice versa. So if the body looses salt, it also looses water. Conversely, if it looses water, it also tends to loose salt.

The Bible refers to salt when it says that we must be the salt of the earth (Matt 5:13). What does this mean to me as a scientist? First of all it means that we must transmit and reflect the beauty and light of Christ. Like normal salt we must allow the full light of Christ to shine through us. How do we do this? It is something God must do in us but we must be willing to be used by God. Like salt we may have to be reformed or recrystallized and being boiled in a solvent can be a painful process. However the Bible says God disiplines those whom He loves (Prov 3:12; Rev 3:19; 1 Cor 11:32; Heb 12:5,6). The word of God also states that God is the potter and we are the clay (Jer 18:6; Rom 9: 21). That implies to me that God is working on us. This theme of God working on us is taken up in Philipians where it says that God will complete the good work that He has begun in our lives (Phil 1:6). God never quits working on us in love because of his compassionate nature.

Secondly like normal salt we should have a cleansing, preserving and healing effect on our neighbours and society in general. We can do this by prayer, being sociable, being there when people in need want you to listen. We can have a healing effect on those around by encouraging them or just by touching them. My belief is that if God took all the saints off this earth anarchy would rule. That is Christians truly devoted to God have a positive effect on their society. That sounds a bit self righteous but imagine the world without Mother Theresa, the Salvation Army, St Vincent de Paul Society, World Vision and many many other such charitable groups. I am sure that there are Christians apart from this group who have a ministry that only God knows of. It may be that they are helping only a single other human being. But that is to what God has called them and they are faithful to that calling. There are people who work unnoticed in the Church for example those working in the creche tending to the young and changing their dirty nappies. These are the unsung heros. Great will be their reward in heaven.

To be the salt of the earth is to be like Christ. That is to be obedient to the Word of God, and to do good and Godly deeds to those in need. Before Jesus began His ministry He was empowered by the Holy Spirit when He was baptized in the Jordan by John the Baptist (Luke 4: 1). It says that the Holy Spirit descended on Him like a dove (Matt 3:16). The Holy Spirit can be symbolized by water . Remember Christ said that out of us shall flow rivers of living water (John 4; 10. 7; 38,39). The living water is the Holy Spirit in our lives. Remember in our bodies, salt and water always go together. As we are doing what Christ wants then the Holy Spirit will be there to guide us. Many who have been used in ministry will agree with this. For example as a new Christian of about 6 months old I was asked to speak to a young person who had been on drugs and was suicidal. In the natural, my mind would have been blank. However that day the words flowed effortlessly in relation to what God was saying about his problem. Anyway that night we went to a Church service and the Pastor in his sermon almost repeated word for word what I had been telling this lad all afternoon. To cut a long story short this lad came to Christ at that service and is still been used by the Lord over 20 years down the track. He got rid of his loaded rifle from his car the following week.

If we operate without the Holy Spirit's guidance then we become like a hyperosmolar (high salt concentration) solution. That is all good intentions but not being led by the Lord or sensitive to His leading. Conversely if we can be full of the Holy Spirit but do nothing when presented with a situation where help is needed. In this situation we are like a hypoosmolar solution (low salt concentration). Remember faith without works is dead (James 2; 17). In both these situations we are responsible for cell lysis or perhaps the spiritual death of the person that we should be helping with God's guidance. How do you know that God is guiding you? The words just flow easily and in a sense while you are talking you know that the wisdom is Godly because you know that you haven't that level of wisdom under normal circumstances. In other words you are learning yourself from what you are saying. This is exactly what is happening to me as this book is written. Hence my feeling that it is God's revelation because it is certainly not of me. Therefore all glory honour and praise is due to God for this book.

In the Bible the second place where salt is mentioned is in relation to Lot's wife (Gen 19). Lot was Abraham's cousin and lived near the twin cities of Sodom and Gomorrah. These towns were very evil places where God's laws were openly flouted. God had had enough of sin in these places and decided to destroy them. The only righteous people were Lot and his family. God sent angels to warn Lot to get his family from out of that place before God destroyed it. The angels also told them not to look back as they left these towns. While they were leaving Sodom and Gomorrah God destroyed these towns. Lot's wife turned back for one last look and turned to a pillar of salt. Lots wife by disobedience lost the presence of water or the Holy Spirit and dried out. Similarly we will dry out in our Christian walk and become ineffective as Christians unless we are obedient to God's leading and secondly are continually filled with the living waters of God's Holy Spirit and his word.

The take home message from this short section is that we should reflect the healing,beauty and flavour of God in our lives. Only God can do that in us if we are willing. Secondly we need the water of the Holy Spirit and his leading in a balanced way if we are to be effective in the ministry of Christ.

CHAPTER 7

THE BODY AS A WHOLE

This final chapter hopefully will illustrate how various tissues in the body cooperate to allow normal functioning of the body as a whole. Breakdown in any one tissue, even to the extent of an impaired single enzyme reaction out of many thousands of good ones in that tissue, will result in ill health.

Let us take a situation where you are placed in imminent danger. For example a car driven by a drunk is coming at you fast. The body responds in a number of concerted ways. First of all your eye or ear sees or hears the danger and relates that danger to your brain. The brain rapidly interprets the danger and then activates the necessary muscles in the body using the nervous system to make you run fast. The pituitary gland located near the brain sends out a hormone called ACTH which is picked by the adrenal gland which is located near the kidney. The adrenal gland after contact with ACTH immediately releases an hormone called cortisol. In addition,the brain stimulates the adrenals to release another hormone called adrenaline. Both hormones then go to the muscle, liver and fat stores to stimulate the breakdown of sugar and fat energy stores. This gives your muscles the necessary fuel to generate the energy containing molecule called adenosine 5-triphosphate or ATP which was referred to in the chapter on gasses. Your lungs cooperate in breathing in more oxygen for this ATP production and your heart beats faster to get the oxygen around the body quicker. The more ATP then the more energy you will have to do the job of running fast. Adrenaline also causes your heart to beat faster so that there is a rapid delivery of oxygen carried by red blood cells to all parts of the body for ATP production. The energy expended and the metabolism associated with this activity generates considerable lactic acid which is the end product of this energy production. To prevent an acidemia or elevated blood acid from occurring the liver converts this lactic acid back to glucose for any further energy needs.

So you see in the process of getting to safety the following tissues cooperate in the body: eyes, ears, heart, lungs, pituitary gland, muscles, nerve cells, brain, red blood cells, liver and adrenal glands. This cooperation is geared toward one thing, that is to get you to safety by supplying the energy required to run fast, jump a fence or whatever to get to safety.

The above example shows how the body preserves itself by removal from a source of danger. The next example shows that the body is able also to heal itself, when subjected to a traumatic insult. In this instance, as in the first, there is a concerted and collaborative effort by several tissues or organs in this healing process occuring after a surgical procedure.

The surgeon's knife has to make a number of cuts in the process of removing a diseased tissue or a tumour. The cut tissues and skin then have to be stitched to prevent any bleeding both internally where the tissues have been cut and externally where the skin has been opened. Despite the skill and care used by the surgeon in this operation it really is the body which is intimately involved in the healing process. Below is a brief description of the events which occur after surgery.

The cells near the cut release substances which close or narrow the blood vessels at the site of the cut in order to stem the blood flow. Platelets, small cells which are in the blood, are attracted to the site of bleeding where they clump together to form a plug at this site. In addition to this mechanism, there are over 20 blood proteins which cooperate with each other to form a fibrin plug around the platelets to further inhibit the bleeding process. The platelets clumping together if you like are analogous to iron mesh and the fibrin plug like cement poured into this iron lattice of clumped platelets.

Most of these plugging proteins are made in the liver and vitamin K is involved in activating several of these proteins. If the body lacks just one of these plugging proteins or is vitamin K or platelet deficient then the clotting process will not function and the person would bleed to death unless there is medical intervention and these missing proteins are replaced through transfusion.

In addition to this elaborate plugging process the cells of the immune system converge on the damaged site to fight off any foreign invaders such as bacteria, viruses, fungi and so on which try to infect the area of the cut (the skin is a great barrier to outside infection). After the bleeding has been stemmed, the body then uses a different batch of proteins to dissolve up the fibrin plug and at the same time promote tissue regeneration and repair. Many growth promoting factors are released by cells at the damaged site (macrophages fibroblasts) which help the skin or tissue to heal the area. Once the damage has been repaired then the proteins used in the healing process are degraded and everything returns to normal. The process of clot removal is called fibrinolysis and is the opposite of coagulation which involves the formation of a clot. Should the body fail to remove this plug or clot there would be an ugly, lumpy scar at the site of the cut. Also with a defective fibrinolytic process we would die of massive clotting processes within the blood vessels of our bodies. So in this healing process we have the involvement of the following cells: Cells lining the cut (epithelial cells), the blood cells such as platelets, white blood cells and the liver which makes the clotting and fibrinolytic proteins. Indirectly the gut cells are involved in absorbing vitamin K for the clotting process. Also the bone marrow is indirectly involved in the coagulation since it produces platelets and white blood cells involved in this process. Also there is a host of hormones and enzymes produced by various tissues in the body to assist in the healing and also to dampen down the trauma associated with this operation.

As already indicated, in the body different tissues not only cooperate with one another but also many communicate with each other. The first example showed how the muscle cells are mobilized by electrical and chemical impulses released from the brain and how the pituitary gland communicates with the adrenal gland by releasing chemical hormone messages. The pituitary gland, which is only the size of a pea, is located directly under the brain. It is the main tissue for sending hormone messages to many other tissues and organs in the body. The pituitary in turn is controlled by another part of the brain called the hypothalamus. The hypothalamus releases factors which causes the pituitary in turn to release some of its hormones. For example the hypothalamus releases thyroid releasing hormone (TRH) which interacts with the pituitary gland causing this tissue to release thyroid stimulating hormone (TSH). TSH then causes the release of thyroxine at the thyroid gland which interacts with and stimulates the metabolism of a number of different cell types within the body. So one factor interacts with a tissue to release another and so on. There is this cell to cell communication going on in the body all the time with various cells chemically talking to each other.

As indicated, the pituitary is the main hormone producing tissue in the body, although other tissues also produce hormones independantly of the pituitary. One of these for example is the pancreas which produces insulin and glucagon both hormones involved in glucose metabolism. An inability to produce insulin results in the cell being unable to take up and thereby metabolize glucose. This results in the disease called Diabetes Mellitus and was discussed in the section on nutrition.

The body has many examples of cells in one part of the body communicating with cells in another. Recent work has shown that cells located next to one another communicate through physical contact. That is, molecules flow backwards and forwards from one cell to another through physical contact of one cell with another. When this cell to cell communication is broken down as it is by substances called tumour promoters then these cells have the potential to become cancerous or malignant. Also when one cell fails to do its job properly then this can effect other cells in the body. For example, in the section on nutrition, we learnt that when the gut cells fail to absorb and metabolize vitamin C efficiently then this can lead to the formation of oxalate stones in the kidney. Thus a malfunction in the gut cells can affect the kidney cells.

In addition to the brain sending out chemical signals or hormones to other tissues in the body many of these tissues also communicate with the brain to let it know whether they require more hormones or to reduce hormone release because the body has sufficient. This process is appropriately known as the feedback loop. For example, as already indicated, TRH is released by the part of the brain called the hypothalamus and interacts with the pituitary gland just below the brain to release of thyroid-stimulating hormone or TSH. TSH interacts with the thyroid gland to then cause the synthesis and release of thyroid hormones, triiodo- and tetraiodo-thyronine or T3 and T4 respectively. T3,T4 and TSH can communicate with the brain to reduce TRH release which in turn inhibits TSH, T3 and T4 release. In other words, the pituitary and thyroid glands can communicate with the brain to tell it what it needs or does not need. It should be stressed that no one organ in the body is autonomous. That is, they all rely on one another no matter how important they may be and this includes the brain. For example, red blood cells and the hepatic and cardiovascular systems feed the brain oxygen, glucose or sugar and purines so that it can do its many functions in turn to help the rest of the body.

The last example of cell to cell cooperatiion is illustrated beautifully by the cells of the immune system. When a foreign microbe enters the body it is digested by cells called macrophages. The macrophage then presents the digested portion of the microbe to cells called T-lymphocytes which cooperate with cells called B-lymphocytes in helping to make a specific antibody against that particular microbe. This antibody then coats the microbe which makes it more appetizing to macrophage cells. The macrophage eats the antibody coated microbe and this eventually results in the demise of this foreign invader.

Should this invader try to enter the body again even years later the body's lymphocytes involved in the initial invasion will remember it and eradicate it even more rapidly. This very briefly is the principle on how immunization works. With immunization, dead bacteria are introduced into the person via injection. Because the bacteria is dead it can cause no harm to the patient. Nonetheless the patient will form antibodies against this bacteria as though it was alive so that if it should try, as a dangerous, live bacteria, to invade this person later on it will be rejected rapidly because the immune system has been primed to fight it through the process of immunization. In other words the cells of the immune system have memory so that a second attack of a microbe is dealt with more rapidly.

In fighting infection there are many cell types involved in the blood. Some of these cells include: T-helper, T-suppressor and B-lymphocytes, macrophages, dendritic cells, neutrophils, natural killer cells, cytotoxic T-lymphocytes. These cells, produced by the bone marrow, are fine tuned in the bone marrow and thymus for their job in life which is to fight infection. The liver supplies nutrients for their growth and the spleen, thymus and lymph nodes help store these lymphocytes to grow and mature. The red blood cells are involved in supplying not only oxygen for their function but also other nutrients (such as purines) not only for their energy needs but also for their needs to multiply and thereby augment their potential to fight infections.

The infection-fighting white blood cells also produce chemicals called cytokines or lymphokines which allows these cells to communicate with each other so that they can grow and mature and eventually destroy any foreign invaders in the body. The suppressor lymphocytes help quieten down the immune system after it has done its job. In autoimmune diseases, lymphocytes attack and destroy the body's own healthy tissues thereby causing disease. Some autoimmune disease are caused by impaired suppressor cell function. Thus suppressor cells can act as a balance so that the immune system does not get out of control. The brain is also involved in controlling immunity in that it can communicate through various neurotransmittors with lymphoid tissues. Conversly the lymphoid system can communicate with the brain by releasing cytokines such as interleukin-1 or other protein messenger molecules which give the brain the signal to increase body temperature as well as other functions. This exciting new field of study is called psychoneuroimmunology, quite a mouthful.

Thus in the overall scheme of immunity, different cells communicate for a common good of restoring health to the body. As indicated, they communicate by touching each other or by sending out chemical signals called cytokines. Everything works in a concerted balanced fashion for the good of the body. In AIDS, the T-helper cells are destroyed by the HIV virus so the whole immune system crumbles and the patient dies of wholescale infection. Antibiotics can give some help to kill bacteria but, without the immune cells working together, infection wins and the patient dies.

Some of the drugs used in transplantation inhibit cell division whereas others inhibit the release of cytokines or chemicals used in cell to cell communication. As a result, the immune system is depressed or suppressed thereby allowing the transplanted organ to survive. Hence these drugs are called immunosuppressive agents.

This whole process of communication between cells and tissues and organs also occurs within or inside the cell itself. For example the nucleus makes a molecule called RNA which is then transported by other proteins to the cytoplasm of the cell. In the cytoplasm this RNA is met by complex proteins called ribosomes in an area of the cell called the rough endoplasmic reticulum. These ribosomes by interacting with the RNA make protein whose structure is determined by the information contained in the RNA. This protein is either used by the cell or is assembled into packages for export out of the cell. This packaging is done in areas of the cells called Golgi bodies. The packaged protein is then transported along the endoplasmic reticulum for export outside the cell. The energy required for this process is made essentially by the mitochondria in the cell. Any foreign or unwanted protein coming into the cell is digested by lysozymes in the cells. So you can see in the normal functioning of the cell that there is cooperation of many subcellular structures within the cell. Without this cooperation the cell would not function and would eventually die. The net result of this cellular non-cooperation would be a very sick person.

In the Bible we hear of the church being the body of Christ (Eph 5: 30; 1 Cor 12: 12-30). Christ is the head and we are the various members making up this body (Coll 1:18; Eph 5:23). Each member, we are told has a specific task. Metaphorically speaking, some members compose the eye to see, some the ear to hear, some the nose to smell and so on. Therefore, in the Church and also in society, each member has a specific function to perform for that church or society to work well.

As the head in the physical sense has a major role to play in motivating the rest of the body as described above, so Christ is the spiritual head of the Church. It is Christ who should therefore direct where His Church will move, when it will move and whatever activities it will get involved in. As frail imperfect humans we need to be following God's directions for all activities.

Different people within the Church are involved in different functions yet they are all under the headship of Christ. The headship on earth of the Church should be sensitive and obedient to the leading of the Lord. It is always a bit risky when only one person hears from the Lord for the rest of the church. Messages from Christ pertaining to moves within the church should be felt in the spirits of the corporate leadership. One must expect some dissension because of the nature of man's intellect but there needs to be a spiritual discernment by the majority of the group. Reliance to God through pray will allow God to communicate what He wants for the Church. And God's communication comes through the spirit or inner being of a person and not the intellect. This is not to decry the role of the intellect which has an important role to interpret what is coming from the inner being.

As indicated, there are many different functions within the Church and we can list some of these. For example some 1.help financially those less fortunate, 2.neutralize erroneous theologies, 3. counsel and help those people with various problems in their lives, 4. assist with the question of ethics and morals, 5. evangelize, 6. look after babies in the church creche, 7. help with children's church, 8. look after the youth, 9. clean the church. So the list goes on. It is not that we have one specific task. For example one can clean the church and can also assist someone or evangelize through the example of their life.

Similarly, cells within the body can also have a multifunctional role such as the red blood cells or the liver. They have a main task to perform but they also do other important tasks as well. One must also be careful not to emphasize one task in importance over another. Sight for example is very important to our normal function but so also is our hearing and proper functionning of our gut tissue. One cannot therefore select one above another. They all have important roles to play and contribute to the overall vitality and functioning of the body. This is all common sense but it needs to be said.

The other important aspect of the Church is that there must be balance. In the Bible, Revelations talks about churches with right theology but not much love whereas others are full of love but the theology is light on (Rev 2,3). Similarly the body needs balance as well. It must have the right proportion of nutrients otherwise it will not function efficiently. For example, if its oxygen intake is not balanced by its excretion of carbon dioxide it will become acidotic. The body must excrete the useless end products of metabolism in order to function properly. Similarly, the Church must rid itself of junk theologies or fads or ignore empty snipes at it by others. It must concentrate on what is positive and nutritious, such as the word of God, for its continued growth and not be side tracked from the role God has designed for it. That is to be an extension of Jesus to the world in order that through us, people within and outside the Church may be set free.

A major weakness we Christians seem to have is a fine tuned ability to criticize others who do not come up to our high and mighty stature. If you have a gripe about a person take it to that person in love and also take it to the Lord in prayer. A body or group full of gossip and innuendo is like a person with an autoimmune disease in which the cells of his body attack one another. The physical body will become diseased and will finally die unless the cells are controlled. Similarly the spiritual body will suffer unless the gossip is suppressed. Nonetheless, the church needs to critically evaluate where it is going. The members need, with God's help, to continually assess their attitudes and repent of the negative ones if they want to be effective like Christ in their lives and ministries. By being more Christ-like we will be more effective in helping and loving one another along life's difficult paths. But we also need to build each other up, not by criticism but by encouragement.

Sometimes one meets well intentioned Christians who get words from the Lord which allows them to criticise others. Those critical words are definitely not from the Lord and in fact they are breaking the third commandment of God (Jer 23:25-40). That is one should not take the name of the Lord your God in vain (Deut 5:11, Exodus 20:7). It is a very serious business to say "God showed me " or "God told me " unless you are absolutely sure. This can also be upsetting because it seems that God is talking to everyone but you. The only words spoken to me from God since 1977, when I gave my heart to him, were "Trust Me". It is usually an impression to do something like write this book. His words give life and encourage us, as they do in scripture. If not then they are probably not from God. They certainly are not from God if they contradict His word in the Bible. So it is very important to discern what the head (Christ) is truly saying to the body (His Church). Wrong messages can upset the body just like a pituitary tumor can do so to our bodies.

Should there be a Christian person who is blatantly living in sin then we, the body of Christ, must tell them in truth and love that sin is both toxic to their spiritual health and their walk with God. If they continue to do so that is their choice. We must always show love to them and not talk of their sinfulness. With prayer and an example of love from us they may return to God's plan for their life. They certainly will not if they are criticised or we assess them in a self righteous way or even use the word of God to show that they are off course. We are responsible mainly for the log removal from our own eye. We are not responsible for other people's attitudes. If any one breaks God's laws then there will be a consequence as sure as breaking any law (for example law of gravity, traffic laws) has its own consequences. The only antidote for breaking God's law is to repent and ask God for His forgiveness.

We are always thankful to God for the well balanced Christians who accepted us in love and who helped through our sorrowful times. Who were a friend when needed. Who were real. Thanks also to God for the Christians who almost screwed my life and walk with Christ. It underlined how fallible we all are. Like the cells in our bodies we need to be sensitive to each other and be Holy Spirit wise in giving the right messages to those who need them.

I'd like to relate a personal story which epitomises what this book and what Christianity is all about. When going through my valley of despair and grief after my wife died, it just seemed that there was no one able to help heal my pain and came to the conclusion that this was part of my cross in life. About 2 months after my wife's death there was a notice in the church mail advertising a grief course. Folks running the course said my condition was too raw to do it. My initial thought was "what a bunch of heartless creatures". Eight months later they rang and accepted me for the course but there was a bit of uncertainty on my part as to whether to do this program as some of the grief had subsided a little (or so it seemed). Eventually enrolment in this course (called Beginning Experience) ensued with the thought that a weekend was probably ruined.

That weekend in October 1992 turned out to be one of the most precious weekends of my life. All the people on this course had experienced grief from the loss of a spouse, including the counsellors. These people opened up their feelings of despair, loss, rejection and anger and, in short, shared their pain openly with one another. Like the cells of the body there was sensitive communication and hugging and healing resulting from these activities. There was just so much crying and healing from long stored emotional pain that weekend with people ministering to one another in their shared grief. Personally so many tears flowed that Monday was taken off as sick leave due to a headache and my eyes were red and swollen.

That weekend was the turning point of my grief and permitted shutting the door on my life and marriage with Denise and to start my life anew. (That door is opened every so often for a little peek back). It was a gradual healing and it took weeks but that weekend was the starting point. God knew my need and got me there with the right people despite my doubts. About 20 months after my wife's death and 10 months after that course I met a lovely person called Heather. We married on June 15,1996, about four and a half years after my wife's death. Unfortunately this relationship dissolved 4 years later due to unresolvable clashes with various family members. This devastated me also.

Where does God come in all this process. First of all He made us and He built into our bodies and spirits the healing process because God is in the business of healing. Just read the gospels or better the whole Bible if you have any doubts. You will find that Christ's total ministry was one of love and healing. In a similar context, Christ uses the love of others to help heal one another. There is so much sung and written about love. My experience is that it is a powerful healing force. I guess this is to be expected since God is love and all those who fully love are in Christ (1 John 4:16-17). By "fully", is meant loving God, our neighbour and ourselves.

God when He made us in His image said that it was very good (Gen 1). Since Adam and Eve first disobeyed God we lost a lot of that "good" that God first described in us. When we came to Christ we were reedemed by His precious blood and our relationship with God reestablished. God has commanded that we must love God, our neighbours and ourselves. Then and only then will we truly live. If we pull ourselves down all the time then we are like an autoimmune disease in which the white blood cells of the body destroy their own tissue. Yes our righteousness is like dirty rags but if we are in Christ then we have the covering of His righteousness and are made worthy (Rom 8:10; Rom 5:18-21; Rom 4:3,22-25). Also there is no condemnation for those who are in Christ Jesus (Romans 8:1).

In this book discussions on the demonic or satanic world have been avoided, mainly because the emphasis has been on the love of God to us through His word and the ministry of His Church. Unfortunately there is a satanic world out there. Jesus many times in the Bible had to deal with it (Mark 9:25-29; Luke 8:28-33; Gen 3:14; 1 Peter 5: 8-9; 1 John 3:8; Eph 6:12). In fact one of the main arms of Jesus' ministry, described time and time again in the gospels, was to set people free from the negative demonic influences which we are bombarded with on mother earth (Luke 4). Satan will try and get into people's lives and then will try to destroy those people in stark contrast to Jesus who gives life in abundance (John 10:10). In the Bible he is described from the very beginning of time as a lier and a murderer (John 8:44). Satan does have a structured army of helpers who are the fallen angels who rebelled with him in Heaven (Matt 25:41; 2 Peter 2:4; Luke 10:17-19; Luke 11:15; Matt 12:24, Eph 6:12). Jesus basically anhiliated the negative forces of Satan and his army by His death and resurrection (Heb 9; Coll 2:13-15; 1 Peter 1:18-19). We have that Christ-derived power if we believe on the Lord Jesus Christ and have faith in what He has gained for us (Matt 10:1; Mark 3:14,15, 6:7, 16:17; Luke 9:1-2; 10:18-20).

The only power Satan has is the power we allow him to have. Satan is a master of deception and gets into people's lives in subtle ways such as through Ouija boards, Tarot cards, seances, dabbling in astrology, fortune telling, NewAge stuff and so on. Before my salvation, games on Ouija boards were part of my recreation. It was after the Ouija games, that my spiritual life started to decline. It was slow but a very definite decline over about 10 years. When coming to Christ, prayer and repentance for playing this "harmless" board game were required for my spiritual detoxification. The solution for being released from any demonic involvement is very simple. Repent of this and any other similar activity and ask God's forgiveness. If you haven't accepted Jesus to be Lord and Saviour of your life then this is the first step for deliverance from satanic influences. As a Christian you can ask the Lord, after repenting, to forgive you and break and heal the influence of Satan in your life. At the same time ask for a full infilling of the Holy Spirit into your life.

You very likely will need the help of a Spirit filled Christian or several church members to help you in this prayer. Repentance from Satanic activity is usually a very quiet pray. Hollywood would have us believe that there is much screaming and frothing at the mouth as shown in the movie "The Exorcist". Sometimes when someone may have become involved in demonic activity in a deep way there may be a bit of a battle. Bye and large it is a quiet process and, after prayer, you come away with the the overwhelming peace of God. There is no more torment, thanks be to God Our Saviour. When you pray and believe in the name of Christ, then Christ will set you free. Fill yourself daily with the Holy Spirit otherwise Satanic forces will try and gain reentry even if your heart is clean (Matt 12: 43-45).

To recap Satan has a body of believers just like there are a body of Christian believers. Satan's army is to kill steal and destroy people's lives whereas God's army is to give life in its full abundance (John 10:10). When you are in Christ Satan should not have any influence in your life. Oh yes, the devil will try and fool you or get friends and other family members to pull you down but just remember that we fight not against flesh and blood but against principalities and powers of darkness (Eph 6:12). So go away and bask in the love of Almighty God and focus on Jesus. Do not waste your life or time pondering Satan.

This spiritual fight that we have with the demonic is similar to attacks that the body has when bacteria and viruses try to enter our tissues. God through immunity has given the body the ability to fight and destroy these microbes. Even though these microbes are invisible to human eyes they are visible to our lymphocytes who recognize and destroy them. When our bodies are run down and in need of rest then these microbes can make us sick. In this situation we go to bed, take antibiotics and eventually our bodies recoup and destroy the infection and we feel well again.

Similarly, Satan and his followers (demons)will try and pull us down and destroy us by guilt, low self esteem or by other subtle devious schemes. Satan generally uses people close to us to try and stuff up our walk with God especially if we are being used in an effective way by God. God however, through the Holy Spirit, has given us the spiritual eyes to discern this invisible demonic activity and to destroy it using the word of God and deliverance prayer. St Paul a spirit filled christian stated he was aware of Satan's devices and advised Christians how to resist him (Eph 2:2; 6:10-17; 2 Thess 3:1-3). Sometimes when we are spiritually weak or sick Satan may gain a temporary upper hand. In this instance we need to turn to Christ in prayer, repent and receive God's forgiveness and meditate on the word of God. Prayer and the Word of God can neutralise these negative spiritual influences. Also when attacked in an area we have been attacked before we are more attuned and immediately reject this additional attack. This is somewhat akin to immunization in that the body will remove a second attack of a microbe much faster because it is primed to do so.

As Christians we need to communicate with and praise God often in prayer. A friend of mine once aptly suggested that prayer is our two way channel between God and us. Prayer is similar to the body communicating with the brain. Remember as said earlier in this chapter, the brain communicates with the body and the body in turn communicates with the brain. We, the body of Christ, need to communicate with our head, Jesus Christ. We need to praise Him for His wonderful goodness as He is the fount of all goodness. This praise is akin to the physical brain receiving sugar and oxygen from the body cells. Christ is more than worthy of our appreciation, praise and thanksgiving. We think of God as being self sufficient, but He needs us because He loves us. By praising God and even quoting the word of God to Him in joy allows full passage for God to minister back to us. This praise of God results in a normal balanced and healthy functionning of the body of Christ.

The other aspect of prayer is that we can tell God of our needs. He knows them but He wants to hear from us just like the physical head need communication about the hormone status of the physical body. By praying God can heal you through your contact with Him. Prayer is a powerful force in our lives and we have the wonderful example of Jesus who often slipped away to a quiet place to communicate with God (Mark 1:35, 6:46; Luke 5:16; Matt 14: 23). In fact it is recorded that Jesus prayed all night to His Heavenly Father (Luke 6:12). We also have the example of many great saints of God who were persistent prayers. People like Mother Theresa, Martin Luther, William Booth, Charles and John Wesley. The list goes on and on. A strong prayer life is the mark of a God fearing, God trusting Christian. To have a close relationship with God we need to talk to him often. It is similar to us communicating with our loved ones. Our relationship with them and our understanding of them grows through communication.

When my walk with God has been a bit weak from time to time it has mainly been because my prayer life has been eroded either by laziness or by the woes and worries of the moment. It is amazing but when you get into sustained prayer and praise to God your worries do not seem as large. Try to give God half an hour in pray daily. It truly will revolutionise your life dramatically. Having a penitent heart is important to an effective prayer life.

Jesus thought prayer was important. He encouraged and taught us how to pray and gave us many examples of His committment to pray (Matt 6;9-13, 26:41; Mark 11:24, 14: 38). If prayer is important to God then it surely is important to us. Prayer keeps the channel open, without it communication becomes blurred. The saying "Seven days without pray makes one weak" is so true.

Coming to the end of this book it seems appropriate to summarize some of the basic tenets in God's word which will result in balance and healing to your life. These basic tenets can be summed up by the words "balanced love".

1. Just as in the body with the head first then other tissues in a certain order being under the head, it is important to have your priorities in the right place. Basically put God (the Head) first then yourself, your family, your job and your ministry. For example if

you are asked to preach in a church (your ministry) and it clashes with your daughter's birthday party (your family) then decline this preaching engagement. Or you may be offered a job which means a substantial promotion but may involve some unchristian activities which may clash with your Christian beliefs then you must put God first and decline this job. It is very important to have your priorities in the right place otherwise you will find your life becoming unbalanced.

2. Love the Lord your God, your neighbour and yourself. The scripture for this also applies to priorities mentioned above (Mark 12:31-33). Sometimes people hurt us and it is easy to harbour resentments which we can justify. However, resentments and grudges will only hurt us (see chapter on Gasses). Let love, repentance and forgiveness dominate and motivate our lives (Matt 6:9-15; 1 Cor 13). Once again put the love of God on the top of your list of loves. But in the loving do not forget to love ourselves. The days of self flagellating or self denigrating Christians is long gone past, thank God.

3. Just as tissues in the body communicate and give to one another, learn to be a giver as you gain blessing from God as you do so (Acts 20:35; Luke 6:38). We live in a time where it seems important to seek pleasure or don't miss out on the "fun things" of life. The television ads blast us with hedonism. For example you will not be happy unless you use a certain makeup, drive a model x car, drink a particular drink and wear type y clothing. We all know too well these things do not make us happy. It is only God's peace which will make us happy as we live according to His plan (John 14: 26-27; Matt 5:3-12).

Also in your life we need to give to ourselves. Golf is my recreation - it is a masochistic streak in me. Seriously the game is enjoyable and it helps recharge my batteries as well as keeping me physically fit. Also it is a great time to pray while you are in the bushes looking for your lost ball. Jesus also went into the wilderness to pray! My mother used to paint when her eyesight was good and my exwife Heather enjoyed folkart. It is all part of loving yourself.

To conclude, the emphasis of this book has been mainly on the nutritive and healing power of the word of God as revealed to us by the

Holy Ghost. God will however use other people in this healing process just like He uses the Medical profession to help heal our bodies. Some of my experiences have been used to illustrate how God moved in my life. In healing my emotions, there was a lot of repentance followed by crying which helped alleviate the emotional pain associated with grief within me. God brought me into the path of Christian people who could help me at that time. As my inner most feelings were exposed to these Christian friends they were able to help me in the area of my emotions just like various cells are involed in healing our damaged bodies. One is eternally grateful to God for their ministry to us all in our hour of need.

As I have said, God knows our needs better than we do and will always make a way. He will shut the doors that need to be shut and open the right ones for us at the right time. It is important that we be healed and whole to help those around us. We must love and accept ourselves before we can love others. If we do not then we need counselling and we need to pray that God will lead us to the right persons who can help us. When you are healed you will know. As Jesus said if you abide in him then you shall be free indeed (John 8:31-32). Finally, to be whole and healed in our Christian walk, we need to be truthful about our pain to God and to others so that they may minister to us. As God said the truth will set us free (John 8: 32). The blessings and healing of God will be in our lives when we continually pray and praise God, repent when needed and when we have the Word of God in our hearts, love God, our neighbour and ourself (Mark 12: 31-33). This three part love and persistent study of the word of God will give a balance to our lives in both the physical and spiritual dimensions.

May God continue to bless and guide you in your walk with Him in Jesus name. Amen.